ESSENTI

MW01168928

BY

ABE MITCHELL

EDITED AND ARRANGED BY

J. MARTIN,
VERULAM GOLF CLUB, ST. ALBANS

NEW YORK
GEORGE H. DORAN COMPANY

ESSENTIALS OF GOLF
— B —
PRINTED IN THE UNITED STATES OF AMERICA

Printing Statement:

Due to the very old age and scarcity of this book, many of the pages may be hard to read due to the blurring of the original text, possible missing pages, missing text and other issues beyond our control.

Because this is such an important and rare work, we believe it is best to reproduce this book regardless of its original condition.

Thank you for your understanding.

Abe Mitchell

TO

SAMUEL RYDER, Esq., J.P.
CAPTAIN OF THE VERULAM GOLF
CLUB ST. ALBANS IN APPRECIA-
TION OF HIS GREAT PRACTICAL
INTEREST IN PROFESSIONAL GOLF

PREFACE

FOR many years past players have been writing to me on various matters appertaining to the game of Golf, but in particular for advice on how to remedy their faults. This book is the outcome of these enquiries.

In it, I have dealt only with what I regard as the essentials of the game. In particular I have endeavored throughout to emphasize the importance of a correct back-swing, which I hold to be of vital importance if a man is to play golf well.

What may perhaps be termed advanced golf has scarcely been touched upon. It is my own experience that the power to make advanced shots, if it is to be an abiding possession, must be acquired by each player through experiment and hard practice, and cannot usefully be imparted by others. Acquired in this way, each advanced shot becomes, as it must do, an expression of the player's individuality.

As their works are available for all to read who so desire, it has not been thought necessary to refer to the methods of play of the great players who have dominated British professional golf for so many years. I should like, however, to take this opportunity to thank them for the encouragement and kindness they have always extended to me since I joined their ranks.

Finally, I have to express my great indebtedness to Mr. Martin for his unfailing help in every stage of the book. He has coöperated with me in planning its scope and in determining the form of each chapter, and also in my endeavor to put clearly before my readers the various steps in what is really a very difficult subject.

I hope that, as it stands, the book will prove useful to all classes of golfers; not only to beginners, but also to experienced players, who may find, as from time to time we all do, that all is not well with their game. To each of my readers I wish the best of luck.

ABE MITCHELL.

St. Albans, England.

CONTENTS

CONTENTS

ILLUSTRATIONS

PUBLISHER'S NOTE

CONTAINED in the reading matter of this book will be found many sketches explanatory of the text.

Other photographic illustrations referred to in the text matter which by reason of mechanical difficulties could not be printed in proper sequence as a part of the text, will be found in an appendix arranged according to number and beginning at page 197.

INTRODUCTORY

CERTAIN terms or expressions are used in this book which it appears desirable to define, to avoid misunderstanding.

1. *Line of Flight:* In Fig. 1, B represents the ball and BA the direction in which it is to be driven. The line of flight is represented by ABC.

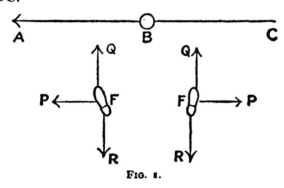

FIG. 1.

2. *Lateral movement:* This is a movement parallel to the line of flight. In Fig. 1 above, the arrows FP represent lateral movements of the feet F.

3. *Forward and Backward movements:* These are movements towards and away from the line of flight respectively. In Fig. 1, FQ would be a forward movement, and FR a backward movement.

4. *Open Face, Shut Face:* These terms are illustrated in Figs. 2 and 3. In Fig. 2 the face of the club is open, in Fig. 3 it is shut. It will

15

be noticed that the open-face is the natural disposition of the club-head, whereas the shut-
face is brought about by turning the left wrist
towards the hole.

5. *Width:* Whenever in the backward swing
the hands make a wide sweep away from the
body the player is said to have got *width*. The
reverse of this sweep would be a narrow swing.

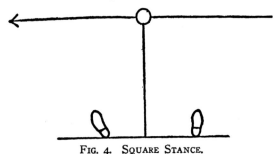

FIG. 4. SQUARE STANCE.

6. *Square Stance:* When the feet are equally
distant from the line of flight the stance is said
to be square (Fig. 4).

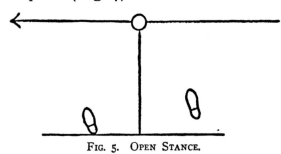

FIG. 5. OPEN STANCE.

7. *Open Stance:* When the right foot is nearer
than the left to the line of flight the stance is
said to be open (Fig. 5).

16

ESSENTIALS OF GOLF

CHAPTER I

ON PRACTICE

IN the evolution of a golfer there are two well-marked stages. In the first stage the player is endeavoring to master the mechanical part of the game, that is to say, to make the strokes; in this stage his attention may be said to be directed to the proper poise of the body, the grip, the pivot, the preliminary movements of the club-head, and so on: in the second stage he is concentrating on making the ball take a certain flight to a definitely desired place. In the former stage he is concerned with what the club-head does before impact, in the latter with its behavior after impact.

Two kinds of practice.—It follows, then, that practice is of two totally different kinds, corresponding with the two stages. In this book an endeavor has been made to deal with the problems that confront the player at each stage, but more especially with those arising in the first stage. These are naturally the more important, for unless he is proceeding along correct lines the player has little chance of reaching the second stage, or, in other words, of ever playing golf at all. It must be remembered that success

19

in golf comes only when the player can make his strokes mechanically and without feeling for them; for only then will he be able to concentrate on the real business of the stroke, which is to send the ball to a certain place in a certain way.

So far as experience and study can teach one there appears to be at least one essential preliminary movement in the making of every golf stroke, and in the following pages the player is shown how this movement can be accomplished. If he masters it, progress in the game becomes possible; if, however, it masters him then no amount of instruction in the rest of the stroke will be of much use. The foundation of each stroke must be right.

It follows, then, that the player must first get his stroke fundamentally correct, and then practice it assiduously until it becomes mechanical. The length of time required to do this depends very largely on the player's natural aptitude and previous experience. If he has swung a club in his childhood his term of trial should be considerably shortened thereby, for old habits soon reassert themselves. If, however, he is taking up golf for the first time after years of cricket and tennis, etc., his progress towards mechanical efficiency will be considerably retarded by the impulses that these games have created; for example the impulse to hit instead of swing, to bend the wrists instead of pivoting, and so on.

With patience all these impulses can be subdued and the player should exercise that patience. We all sally forth into match play and competitive golf much too early and much too often; we ought to keep pegging away in remote corners of the course, for it is only in this way that the foundations of real success can be laid. Great musicians spend countless hours in acquiring and perfecting their technique before they pass on to interpretation, and the golfer should take a lesson from them.

Golf a mental game.—To all players who read this book and propose to put into practice its teaching, a word of advice, and perhaps of encouragement, is necessary. Golf, it must be remembered, is a mental game. Before a stroke is played a clear mental picture should be formed of what it is intended to do, and this is as essential in practice as in actual play. The fact that the occasion lacks seriousness does not diminish the urgency for clear thinking in all spells of practice; indeed, failure to progress is generally due to inability to concentrate and seldom to actual physical shortcomings.

When a player is endeavoring to correct a fault it is very probable that rhythm, timing, etc., will be at fault. This is inevitable, for the mind is not concentrating on the swing as a whole but only on one particular section of it; most especially, of course, is this true when some fundamental error is under review. The success or failure of the practice is not to be judged solely, if at all, by ball flight; often some of the most effective work appears to be giving discouraging results. If, however, the player refuses to be dismayed and continues so to discipline his mind that the "corrective movement" gradually assumes its proportionate place in the mental picture of the stroke then the rhythmic swing will reappear—this time, it is to be hoped, on correct lines.

So far note has been taken only of those practices that are concerned with the mechanical swing and which in many cases scarcely need the presence of a ball at all. Regarding the practice of those whose game is already on correct lines there is little need to say anything. The attention is riveted in such cases on what it is intended the club-head and ball shall do after impact and the player is himself the best judge of the success of the shot for he alone knows what the object of the shot was. But even in this case improvement will not come unless the mental picture is clear so that the muscles can be properly directed and controlled. This is the second stage mentioned earlier in this chapter; until this stage is reached the player can hardly be said to be playing golf.

Practice Hints.—In all spells of practice it is good policy to begin with the mashie. It always

22

takes time to get the eye attuned and the muscles in nice working order, and this can be done most expeditiously and with least exasperation by practicing chip shots round a green. In such a case bad timing and faulty swinging do not involve a tithe of the waste of time and patience that would follow on foozles, slices and pulls with the long-distance clubs.

But apart from considerations of economy it is highly desirable when practicing the long shots to have acquired first of all a sense of ball control, and the mashie practice should have been sufficiently prolonged for this sense to be acquired. It is impossible, in fact, to overestimate the need for this feeling of ball control when the driver or brassie is in the hand, for the mind will be sufficiently occupied with those other aspects of the drive that are in themselves quite enough to be going on with.

The mashie practice, at this stage, should be the ordinary pitch and run shot in which the swing and body movement, etc., are quite straightforward. If a player includes practice at the cut shot or any other advanced stroke requiring exceptional club and wrist movement he is really not helping himself much towards rhythmic driving later; indeed he will undoubtedly undo much of the advantage gained by the other form of mashie practice. If he wishes to attempt such shots he should defer the practice until after the driving spell is over.

23

He would probably do well to defer it altogether.

Mashie.—Practice with the mashie should commence with chip shots round a green. A caddie is really a hindrance at this stage for the player will want to see what the balls do after they pitch, whereas the caddie will be apt to start picking them up before they have stopped rolling, and to distract the attention of the player in other ways. Deep concentration is required. The player must keep vividly in his mind what exactly he wants the ball to do: that is, he must visualize the ball's trajectory, the spot it shall drop on, and its subsequent behavior. The feeling of mastery will repay him for this mental effort.

As the practice proceeds the length should be gradually increased until a two-thirds shot is reached: this should be the limit. It will probably be noticed that this length has hitherto been looked upon as a full mashie shot. From this point balls should be dropped at intervals back to the starting point and then played in succession to the green. The gradual increase in length will scarcely be perceptible to the player and thus he will not lose the "controlled swing motif" that it is so desirable he should maintain; played in the reverse order, with the long shot first, the tendency would be to over-swing. It makes each shot appear more like an entirely new prop-

24

osition if the grip is taken afresh for each stroke.

There are many ways of playing the mashie, and the approaches to greens are also varied: flat, hummocky, uphill, downhill, slanting, hard, soft and so on. The appropriate shot for each of these approaches should be practiced until, when any green is approached, the best type of shot to be played should come automatically to the mind. Every player knows how disastrous it is to change one's mind at the top of the swing, to make, say, a back-swing for a pitch-and-run and a down-swing for a pitch. The way to avoid a recurrence of this is constant practice at that type of shot that the player has found to be the best and safest for that particular approach.

When the player has run through his range of shots he should begin to vary the lies. At once the type of shot to be played will be changed and the player may find a use for some of the shots dealt with in Chapters XV, XVII and XXI, which his previous practice had perhaps not included. All these shots should be played from different lengths: in this way it will be found that some of the shots are not advisable for any but quite short lengths.

Iron.—Practice with the iron should proceed along somewhat similar lines. The player should begin with a full mashie length and continue practicing at that length until the ball is well under control. The length should then be increased gradually until a three-quarter swing is reached. This should be the limit. From that point balls should be dropped at a few yards' interval back again to the starting point and then played in succession to the green just as was done in the case of the mashie.

It would be as well for the player to try a few full irons: in all probability he will find that he has gained nothing on the three-quarter swing but has lost in both direction and ball control. It should be the aim to play only controlled shots with both iron and mashie because great accuracy is usually required and this entails great concentration. Although it may appear quite a wrong thing to say, yet it is undoubtedly easier to concentrate and to achieve a desired object with a partial swing than with a full one.

If the player has achieved a measure of ball control with both iron and mashie he will have discovered that it is the close-lying ball that lends itself most to that object and the perched-up ball the least.

Wooden clubs.—A caddie is indispensable for practice with wooden clubs, for otherwise there is an irresistible tendency to lift the head to mark the ball: in addition this means that the player cannot give undivided attention to the making of the shot that he has in mind. The caddie should be so placed that the sun is lighting up the approaching ball: it saves time and prevents accidents.

In driving spells it is essential to select a place to aim at—a green for preference—and to keep this in mind when coming on to the ball. Haphazard driving is all against mental discipline, and therefore against progress. Good strokes are good only if they represent a successful but conscious effort at placing.

If a wind is blowing, the player should get practice at driving at all angles to it and not be satisfied unless and until the ball is behaving as expected.

Begin brassie or spoon practice with encouraging lies and endeavor merely to get them up and keep them straight. Don't go all out; the object should be to swing accurately and to time the wrist action successfully—in other words, to acquire ball control. As a further test of progress he should try a few slices and pulls, and if these are successful a good bang or two might be made to finish the spell with the good lies.

Next practice playing the balls from bad lies; by this time the eye is steady and the temptation to hit subdued, and as good command has been gained over the wrists the results should be encouraging.

Once a player realizes that, provided he does not get flustered, he can brassie out of bad lies and get the ball up, he will have little difficulty in doing this when a serious game is in progress. All spells with the spoon should aim at acquiring a controlled finish. For this purpose it is best to approach a green. Players are advised not to waste time by practicing with the wrong clubs for certain lies and lengths: this is not only a waste of time but it tends to weaken the stroke habit that they should be endeavoring to acquire.

CHAPTER II

CHOICE OF CLUBS

THE proper person to advise on the choice of clubs is the club-professional, as he knows best the build and physical powers of the player. All that one can do here is to lay down general rules and give the reasons for doing so.

Weight.—It is inadvisable to play with light clubs. Light clubs, through their lightness, induce in a player the desire to hit, whereas the object to be attained is a rhythmic swing. Therefore the heavier the head within reason the more effectually will the "swing motif" be implanted in the mind. "Let the club-head do the work," is a good motto, for it leads to a good follow through.

Shaft.—Hard hitters need stiffer shafts than their fellows. For the medium hitter, however, all shafts except those of the mashie, mashie-niblick and niblick should have a fair amount of spring in them. The ideal club has a minimum of wood in the shaft, and the "give" extends up to the grip. Whippiness in the shaft is not a matter of personal liking at all: if it were, it would not be worth mentioning. Stiff shafts have the effect of making the hands creep to the right so that the left is too much on top and the right too far under. The result of this change of grip is that in the back-swing the arms and hands hug the body and the swing is confined. In other words the fling movement is hindered and there is little width in the swing (*see* Back-swing, p. 40). Usually the right hand lifts, and instead of the proper pivot a see-saw movement of the shoulders is induced; that is, the left shoulder drops and the right rises in the back-swing while in the down-swing the reverse of this movement takes place. In a word, the stiff shaft seems to communicate some of its own stiffness to the player.

As regards length of shaft the driver at any rate should not be curtailed, for, with the ball teed up and a level stance, accuracy of swing is not a difficult matter, while the lengthy shaft gives one an intensified feeling of the club-head.

The brassie and spoon being needed for more accurate work should be slightly shorter in the shaft. As regards the iron clubs it might be said here that a short shaft lends itself to more accurate work and tends to prevent an improper use of the club.

Grips.—A grip that admits of treatment with wax, resin or any of the preparations made for the purpose, is the best. Rubber grips soon wear out and are useless in wet weather. It is an advantage if the upper half of the grip be thickened so that the left hand can hold more

30

firmly: especially is this desirable in the winter months when the fingers are apt to be numb.

Care of Clubs.—Opinions differ about the wisdom of polishing up the blades of iron clubs, but there can be no two opinions regarding the unwisdom of neglecting the shafts. In these days good shafts are all too scarce and every one ought to do his utmost to preserve those he is fortunate enough to possess.

Wet clubs should be dried at the conclusion of a round and rubbed with a little oil, rather than dried artificially. In the hot season an occasional rubbing with oil is desirable to keep the wood from splitting.

In some Golf Clubs there is a commendable practice of entrusting the care of clubs to the professional staff. The saving to the player of such an arrangement far exceeds the small annual charge that is usually made.

Chapter III

THE DRIVE—PRELIMINARIES

On the tee the player has an opportunity of playing a stroke under ideal conditions. He is not hurried, the ball may be teed, and he has a reasonable space in which to find a level stance.

These are important advantages, but there are other considerations that are more important and far-reaching in their consequences, and it is to be feared that many of us are apt to pay undue heed to these. These are the method of gripping the club, the disposition of the feet relative to the line of flight and the general bracing up or preparation of the muscles for the work that has to be done.

The player, then, is urged to take great heed to the advice given on these heads both in this chapter and throughout the book.

The Grip

The left arm is the important arm in golf, and the method of gripping with the left is profoundly important. Although golf is a two-handed game it is desirable, as far as possible, so to grip with the hands that they work as one.

The following instructions apply to the grip

for all clubs except the mashie. For certain shots with the mashie the grip is modified (*see* pp. 118, etc.).

Left-hand.—Two knuckles should be showing. All four fingers should be gripping firmly but especially the first two. The thumb should be placed only slightly on the side of the shaft and should be pressing hard so that the ball is quite taut. The thumb grip should be even firmer than that of the fingers.

Right-hand.—The hollow of this hand should fit over the left thumb and the right thumb should lie slantwise across the shaft. This hand should so hug the left that the little finger overlaps the first finger of the left. The grip of this hand is quite light. Care must be taken to see that the thumb and first finger lie side by side on the shaft: if not there is a tendency for the hand to slip about and be in a wrong position when the time comes for it to take an active part in the stroke (Figs. 6-11).

STANCE

(Figs. 12-15)

Feet.—An almost square stance is desirable, that is, the two feet and shoulders should be in a line almost parallel to the line of flight. The right foot should be a little nearer the line of flight than the left and should be square to it. If a line be drawn from the ball at right angles to the line of flight it should pass just behind the left heel. In this position the player is able both to swing widely in the back-swing and to follow through widely in the down-swing. If the right foot be much advanced so that the player tends more and more to face the hole the back-swing will be a confined movement but there will be a good follow through; on the other hand if the right foot be withdrawn the back-swing will be wide and free but the follow through will be curtailed.

Weight.—The right foot carries slightly more weight than the left: in each case the weight is on the ball of the foot and not on the heels. As a matter of fact the heels are unresponsive to muscular impulse whereas the toes are alive. This means that the head is well forward, in fact it should be so much so that the center of gravity should almost appear to be between the line of the feet and the ball. This is very important if the back-swing is to be free and the player is to find himself comfortably poised at the top of the swing; for the momentum of the club-head in the back-swing cannot be successfully counter-balanced in any other way.

Arms and Shoulders.—The right shoulder is lower than the left owing to the lower grip. The left arm is straight and the right elbow is hugging the body. The left shoulder top has a tense feeling whereas the muscles of the right arm and shoulder are relaxed. This difference

34

in tautness is the direct result of the difference in the strength of the grips of the two hands.

In taking up the stance the club should be grounded first, and the hands dropped so that the left arm is fairly close to the body. There will thus be a distinct angle between the line of the shaft and that of the fore-arm: in fact the shaft may actually be so low that the club is grounded on the heel only. Although this is perhaps not desirable yet it is an error in the right direction. Certainly if the shaft be inclined more vertically this can only be done by arching the wrists and bringing both arms away from the body which would be fatal to the back-swing. In such a case both arms would lift, the right elbow would stick out and there would be little, if any, pivoting. At best only a stiff-armed chop-shot would result.

Right Knee.—Finally, the right knee should bend forward towards the line of flight and inwards towards the ball. This is very important, as the initial movements in the back-swing, which have for their object a wide fling of the club-head and hands, are most effective if the right knee is bent in this way.

35

CHAPTER IV

THE DRIVE—BACK-SWING

(Figs. 16-28, also 41-67)

THE principles laid down in this chapter are of
the utmost importance. They apply to the full
swing with all the clubs and therefore the player
will do well to ponder them very carefully.

When a first-class player is driving, the spec-
tator, no matter how observant he may be, is
unable to distinguish between the movements
that are deliberate and those that are, as it were,
incidental. Consequently many failures to make
correct or satisfactory swings are directly traceable to concentration on the wrong points.

Accordingly in this and the next chapter an
attempt is made to give the reader a peep into
the player's mind. A distinction is drawn between the essential and unessential movements,
and instructions are given in the order in which
they appear to be necessary. For additional
clearness they are numbered, although it will
readily be recognized that some of the numbered
movements are really simultaneous. Recogniz-
ing that there are, roughly, two classes of players, beginners and adepts, the instructions have
primarily in mind the first class, but a summary,

36

putting the matter in another way, is added for the guidance of those who can take a comprehensive view of the golf swing and, having got the essentials right, need only some condensed formulæ to keep them right.

As a number of rules are apt so to confuse the player that he can hardly see the wood for the trees, it should be said at the outset that for the beginner the back-swing is the important part of the golf swing, and that in the back-swing the most important movement is the lateral movement of the hips. If this is kept steadily in mind, the other instructions will be more likely to assume their proper importance.

PLAYING INSTRUCTIONS

Having taken up his stance as already suggested, with hands and head well down, left shoulder raised and braced, and the weight on the ball of the foot, the player should proceed as follows:—

1. *Turn the right hip very slightly forward towards the ball.*

This should be the actual initial movement of every golf shot. It is really very slight and has the effect of pushing the hands slightly forward but not the grounded club-head. In the gymnasium this would be called a complementary movement, a term applied to all movements that precede and directly lead up to the primary or actual movement that it is desired to make. Al-

37

though apparently a trivial matter it is really quite important and should be the initial movement in all except bunker-shots. Some players substitute a waggle for this movement as they recognize that rhythm cannot readily be secured, if at all, from a stationary position.

2. *Keeping the head still, make a lateral movement of the hips to the right, parallel to the line of flight and brace the right leg (see 5 below, also Figs. 16-26).*

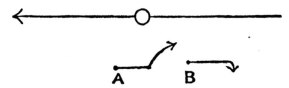

FIG. 21.—SHOWING THE CORRECT MOVEMENT OF THE HIPS—A AND B—IN THE BACK-SWING.

This has the effect of transferring more weight to the right foot, and of raising the right hip and shoulder while lowering the left. The lowering of the left facilitates the passage of the arms across and beneath the body and so maintains the balance.

These instructions might almost have been expressed by saying "straighten the right leg." Some players, however, might merely transfer the weight to the heel, which is specially to be avoided; others might fail to get this hip movement through omitting to bend the right knee in the stance.

3. *Simultaneously with the hip movement*

38

drag the club-head backwards along the line of flight.

The hands are ahead of the club-head in this movement and, in order that they may lead, the left elbow must hug the body: the left wrist is bent towards the ball. This is the beginning of what is really a backward fling of the club-head, and it is important that this should be noted at the outset as the remainder of the swing will be more readily visualized.

4. *From the moment the hips are moved laterally until the beginning of the down-swing brace the right leg and side.*

The importance of this cannot be overstated. The weight has been thrown largely onto the right sole but not the heel. If there is a con-

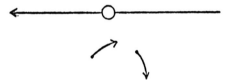

FIG. 22.—SHOWING INCORRECT HIP MOVE-
MENTS IN THE BACK-SWING.

scious pressure on the heel there must have been a double movement of the right hip, viz. laterally and backwards, really a sweep of the hip away from the line of flight (Figs. 21-22). This, of course, is wrong. There must be no further movement of the right knee, and the muscles of the calf, thigh, and up the inner side of the leg must all be braced—fighting, as it were, to prevent the body from swaying backwards under

39

the momentum of the club-head. The right foot will be pressing firmly and the toes will be tending to curl up in keeping with the general tenseness. Only the inner part of the sole of the left foot will carry any weight, the heel being slightly raised. The right foot should be at right angles to the line of flight, not pointing outwards, for this will help to check the tendency both to sway back and to twist the right hip away from the line of flight. *There should be no turning of the shoulders until this lateral movement of the hips has been made.*

5. *When the right leg begins to brace, lift the hands in a wide sweep keeping the head down.*

If the wrists have not been stiff the uplift of the hands will have the effect of throwing the club-head upwards and around the body to its place above the right shoulder. The mind should be riveted in this movement on the task of making the club-head continue along the line of flight as long as possible; the wider the sweep both of hands and club-head the better. (*See* Full Swing, p. 56.)

If the weight has been kept well forward on the toes, and the head down, the swing of the club-head should not upset the balance. The swing backwards of the hands will have had the effect of bringing the shoulders round and also the left hip will have been dragged inwards towards the ball. The backward passage of the

40

arms is stopped by the left shoulder and not by the wrist muscles. There will be a feeling of great tenseness along the left arm. The extent to which the left shoulder turns is determined by the extent to which the right hip twists before it locks. When locking takes place all the muscles from that hip across the back are braced in an endeavor to hold the left shoulder. The player should feel well braced, with the swing well under control. Indeed, while the left shoulder is following the hands the brace of the back muscles should practically be a conscious endeavor to twist the left shoulder in the opposite direction towards the hole. If this is not done the arms have no firm origin to work from. This is the prime cause of most of the spells of short, labored driving that many of us go through from time to time, for virtually the body is cut out.

CHAPTER V

THE DRIVE—DOWN-SWING

(Figs. 29-68)

IN the last chapter we left the player at the top of the swing. The position was one of great tenseness. The right leg from the knee downwards was taut and endeavoring to resist a further backward sway: above the knee the hip had rotated slightly, away from the hole, and there was no bending at the knee. The head was down and as far forward as was possible without upsetting the balance. Little weight was on the left foot, and the left leg and side were relaxed. The left shoulder had come round and down and was under the chin, and the left arm was tense from the shoulder to the hands (Figs. 27 and 28).

Across the back from right hip to left shoulder the muscles were tense and at attention, so much so that the slightest twisting at either knee or hip would cause a corresponding movement in the upper part of the body (Fig. 29). The left hand was gripping very tightly and the right slightly less so. Both elbows were bent, the left only slightly, and were near together. The left wrist was not under the shaft and both wrists were resisting the backward swing of the club-head without breaking or bending.

The downward swing is, in a sense, much less complicated; at any rate the important points are easier to grasp and carry out. Speaking broadly, the movements are the reverse of those in the back-swing. The player should proceed as follows:

1. *Slowly but firmly unwind at the hips by a forward and downward movement of the right hip and a rotary and upward movement of the left hip.*

This movement is really the reverse of the hip movements in the up-swing. It is accompanied by a slight lowering of the body towards the ground and a splaying of the knees (*see* notes to Figs. 41-67). The hip movement will be in advance of the shoulders, and when the left heel comes back to earth the left leg should be braced. The left leg below the knee is now taut, and fighting against the tendency of the body to come forward. Above the knee the rotary movement of the thigh and hip continues now as a twist, getting the left side out of the way, as it were, of the stroke (*see* pp. 49-50).

The rotary hip movement brings the shoulders round: it will thus be seen that the shoulder movement is quite involuntary and need not be given a thought.

As the left arm is coming with the left shoulder, and the left shoulder with the braced hips, the player may be said to be making a sling with

43

hips. This slinging movement of the hips is one of the secrets of the long ball (*see* p. 71).

2. *Simultaneously with the unwinding of the hips bring the hands downwards close to the body with firm wrists.*

There is great wrist compression at the top of the swing and the rebound of the club-head should have begun before any conscious wrist movement takes place. The grip should be firm with the left hand, and the third and fourth fingers should specially tighten up.

It is a help to the player to remember that the club should trace out the same path in the down-swing as in the up-swing. It is important to bring the hands downwards towards the feet and not outwards towards the line of flight, for by so doing a complete follow through is made possible.

While the hands are returning to the address position the right foot is contributing its last effort in the swing by supplying the prop or stay, but by the time the hands are in front of the body the left heel is on the ground and the weight is mainly on the left foot. The left arm is now at full stretch and the right elbow is hugging the body—the right palm and wrist facing the hole. In a word, the player is back again in the position of the address with this difference, that the club-head is moving and the weight is on the left.

It should be noted that in both the back and

44

downward swings the club is swung by the left hand and that, in fact, the left shoulder is the center of rotation. The less the right is allowed to do between the commencement of the stroke and the moment of impact the better. If in the back-swing the right overpowers the left the fling will become a lift, the back-swing will be curtailed, and the stroke will lose width. Similarly in the down-swing, if the right is, at the beginning, the predominant hand, the club-head will lag behind and will be too late in getting into the line of flight of the ball: the left elbow will be bent and both power and direction will be lost. The right hand should not actively come into the stroke until just before impact.

3. *At impact throw the hands forward and roll both forearms over towards the hole.*

At the moment of impact the club is at right angles to the line of flight, and if the club-head subsequently gains on the hands before the ball has left it a slice will result. Therefore the hands must go forward and, in addition, the grip of both hands should be fierce so as to overcome the inertia of the ball. The club-head should be in contact with the ball as long as possible and should travel along the line of flight as far as possible.

Again, after impact, the club-head naturally tends to rise. The forward movement of the

45

hands delays this. If, however, the club-head rises quickly the face will gradually tilt back skywards and the ball will have too lofty a trajectory (Fig. 32).

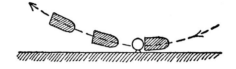

FIG. 32.—SHOWING CLUB-HEAD RISING QUICKLY AFTER IMPACT, TILTING THE FACE AND PRODUCING A LOFTED SHOT.

To avoid this the forearms are steadily rolled over and if, at the same time, the hands are moving forward the club will not only be keeping in the line of flight but the face will continue to move at right angles to the ground. In this way the trajectory of the ball is lower and the flight longer. Such a ball is more under control; it has a longer carry and only a short run (Fig. 33).

FIG. 33.—SHOWING THE FLATTER ARC AND UNTILTED CLUB-FACE WHEN THE FOREARMS ARE ROLLED AT IMPACT.

It should be noted that the blow is delivered mainly with the right and that the chief function of the left has been to guide the club-head so that, at impact and after, the right may be employed most advantageously and effectively.

46

IMPORTANT POINTS TO REMEMBER

So far the player has been instructed only in what he has to do, and it remains to enumerate a few of the more important points to be remembered in carrying out these instructions.

Right Elbow.—This should hug the body. If it is stuck out and bent, the forward fling of the hands and the roll of the forearms are impeded.

Left Elbow.—If this elbow be bent and stuck out from the body the stroke is spoilt for two reasons:—

(*a*) The bent arm will "give" when the blow is delivered, whereas it must be firm and taut: in fact the hands should gain on the elbow.

(*b*) The fling of the hands, although really from the left shoulder, should be partly the result of rolling the forearms over, and this cannot be done unless the left elbow is behind the hands during the turning movement. A short sliced shot usually results from a bent left elbow (Fig. 28).

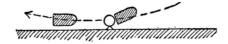

FIG. 34.—SHOWING THE SMOTHERING EFFECT
OF ROLLING THE FOREARMS TOO SOON

In practicing the down-swing the rolling movement may start too soon: if so, a smothered shot, scuttling off to the left, results. The club face in this case is overhanging and the toe has come forward (Figs. 34, 35). This is the commonest form of faulty timing, and players are apt to become discouraged too readily by such topped foozles. Confidence will come by continued practice and the growing feeling of power will reward the player for his patience.

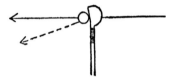

FIG. 35.—SHOWING THE TOE OF THE CLUB BROUGHT UNDULY FORWARD THROUGH MISTIMING THE ROLL OF THE FOREARMS.

It is this lack of confidence that is the cause of so many curtailed follows-through, there being a fear that the roll of the forearm will send the ball to the uttermost rough. It usually does if the player is not in the habit of alternating his matches with spells of practice.

Shoulders.—At impact the left shoulder should be well up so that the left arm can be fully extended. Indeed this shoulder should never be consciously dipped at any part of the swing.

The strong right is always tending to butt in, and unless the left shoulder is up the power of the left arm is weakened and the right takes control in an endeavor to get length. There can be little follow-through in that case and there is an alarming tendency to sway forward. If the mind be concentrated on swinging the left, giving it ample time at the top of the swing to change direction and coöperate with the return

48

spring of the wrists, the right will fulfill its proper rôle of sleeping partner. A player who is dipping his right shoulder in the initial half of the down-swing is on wrong lines; for he is struggling prematurely to get in a powerful blow with his right. That shoulder should be dipped later when the follow-through is being made round the rigid left leg.

Weight.—At impact and during the follow-through the weight should be behind the ball. The club-head cannot be flung forward unless the left foot and leg are firm and the body is held well back. The swing after impact is round the left leg. If it should "give" there is nothing to swing against, power goes out of the swing effort and the stroke goes astray. Therefore give the left leg a chance by hanging well back. This does not mean that the weight should be on the right. That would be no good at all; the right cannot hold the body back, nor can a down-swing be made round it. The weight will be almost entirely on the left, and if that leg be braced and the muscles of the left side as well, there is little to fear. The right shoulder will appear to the onlooker to be doing the lion's share of the hitting, for it will have come round after the hands. This is really so, and at the same time it is a sure sign of good driving, for it means that the left shoulder has remained firm so that the right could follow through only by the body turning and facing

49

the hole. If the left shoulder had moved laterally through the leg giving, the right would have moved laterally also and there would have been little turning of the shoulders (*see* Drive. Figs. 41-68).

It appears to be a cardinal truth, in considering the rigidity of the left shoulder, both at the top of the swing and at impact, that there can be little power in an arm movement if it is actuated from an unbraced center. Both at the top and at impact the left shoulder is held firmly; by the back muscles in the former case, and by a rigid left side in the latter. The reader has need only to put this book down and swing his left arm backwards and forwards, first with the muscles concerned relaxed, and then braced, to convince himself of the truth of this.

One is driven to the conclusion that much of the poor driving to be seen, sadly lacking in power, is due to a relaxed left shoulder at the top, which necessitates a too early application of the right. Subconsciously we know that the right is a good friend, a reserve of power, and with a relaxed back-swing leaving the left shoulder unsupported and feeble, the right takes command at once with the result that its power, centered largely in the wrist, is dissipated too soon. The rolling of the right wrist, which should have been reserved to keep the club-head in contact with the ball after impact, cannot now be effected. Further, the club-head has generally reached such a position at impact that any further wrist movement by the right will send the ball astray. A swing of this kind is characterized by a bent left elbow, a hurried down-swing and an absence of follow-through (Figs. 36-9).

FINAL HINTS ON THE SWING

1. *Hang on throughout with the fore part of the grip and the fore part of the feet.*
2. *Have the feeling in the back-swing that the club-head describes this path before it is lifted.*

FIG. 39A.—SHOWING IMAGINARY PATH OF CLUB-HEAD REFERRED TO IN HINT 2 ABOVE.

3. *Imagine you are cracking a whip at the ball, or whipping a top.*
4. *Swing back against the resistance of the ball of the right foot.*
5. *Swing down against the resistance of the ball of the left foot.*
6. *In the beginning of the down-swing let the left knee splay a little towards the hole, but straighten it at impact.*
7. *Keep the chest facing the line of flight until the hands have swung under and through the ball.*

51

CHAPTER VI

THE SWING AS A WHOLE

(Figs. 41-68)

The Mental Picture.—Having now been instructed in the details of each section of the swing, it remains for the player to apply his mind to the task of visualizing the swing as a whole. This is by no means an easy thing to do, for so long as he is mainly concerned in acquiring mechanical proficiency, as he must be in the early stages, he will necessarily have but a dim mental picture of the stroke as a whole.

As he progresses, however, the mechanical part of the swing will gradually absorb less and less of his attention until in time he will acquire the essential power to think of two things at once, namely, of the swing as a whole, and of each individual part of it as it comes along. How long it will take him to do this depends on the seriousness with which he tackles the game. But until he can perform this two-fold feat, little headway is possible.

Progress in the development of a golfer resembles very much that of a child learning to read. In the early stages the child is so engrossed in the task of spelling out the words of a sentence

52

that he fails to comprehend its meaning. But as time goes on his reading powers develop. Some words he can pronounce quite readily as he has become familiar with them, and this ready association of word with word enables him to sense the meaning of what he is reading. Eventually, as we know, he is actually able to grasp the meaning of a passage before he gives vocal expression to the individual words. And further, the more readily and clearly he can thus see ahead, the more effectually can he stress the words and so bring out fully and clearly their real meaning. Until he can do this, he cannot be said to have mastered the art of reading.

In the same way a golfer begins by endeavoring to master each section of the swing without reference to the whole. Presently some of the details, like some of the young reader's words, can be carried out without mental effort, until eventually he may reach the stage when he can frame the whole swing in his mind so clearly that his body, like the little boy's tongue, can be made to give correct expression to this mental concept.

If he cares to pursue this analogy further, the reader of this book will see other points of similarity between the pupils learning to read and those learning to play golf. But the essential point that it is desired to emphasize here is that the golfer, if he is to play well, must see the swing as a whole both before he makes it and while he is making it.

Now we can divide the young reader's experience into two parts, the first of which ends with the probationary period from which he emerges as a finished elocutionist. In the golfer's case, we may use the parts of the swing to indicate the corresponding stages. In the probationary stage he is concerned largely with the back-swing, and in the second stage with the down-swing, but more particularly with that part of it that immediately precedes and follows impact (Fig. 40).

FIG. 40.—SHOWING THE SECTIONS OF THE GOLF SWING WITH WHICH THE BEGINNERS (a) AND ADEPTS (b) ARE MOSTLY CONCERNED.

Braced Left Side.—Every golfer knows that the body responds very readily to any train of thought that may be suggested by circumstance. If, for example, the player's mind is dwelling on a bunker instead of the green beyond, it is in the bunker that his ball will most probably come to rest. There are unscrupulous players who know this, and actually endeavor to influence adversely the play of their opponents by drawing their attention to such trouble as they are preparing to strike.

But this principle of suggestion can also be used by the player for his own benefit if he cares to concentrate on what it is advantageous to do.

54

It may be said here, and will be repeated again in the chapter on Length, that every golf stroke must be thought out clearly beforehand so that the muscles may be warned, as it were, in advance of what they are expected presently to do. One cannot expect a ready response to a mental effort that does not begin until the swing, such as it is, is half-finished. The following advice, therefore, is worth serious consideration.

First of all, the player should visualize the place on the fairway to which he wishes the ball to fly. This mental picture will help him to go through with the stroke after impact, and so put the proper finishing touch to his wrist work.

In the second place, when bracing up the left shoulder in the address, he should let his mind dwell for a moment on the thought that at impact the whole left side should be braced. This "impact" feeling, if we may so term it, will steady his back-swing by preventing his shoulders and arms from getting right back before the hips have got going. But its chief value lies in the influence that it will exert on the swing as a whole. For example, it will make the player think throughout of the position of the clubhead. Then the fact that the left leg has to be braced to withstand it, will remind him that this is the point when the great swing-forward effort is to be made, and so will influence him to defer it until that point. Also, a firm left leg will be opposed to the forward tendency of the body;

55

thus there will be a definite purpose in the body effort of the down-swing. It is in the down-swing that so many seasoned players go wrong—or rather, it is in their conception of their down-swing that the whole effort is ruined. The back-swing and the first part of the down-swing seem, in such cases, to be full of purpose, but the stroke is practically spent at impact, and a poor weak blow results. The player's mental picture of the swing ended at the ball and his muscular effort ended even earlier. That was the root cause of the swing petering out. The mental vision must start at the ball and must extend beyond it, if this state of things is to be remedied. It is a question of purpose after all.

The back-swing should be slow. Watch one of the great players. The backward swing is slow and deliberate and carries no suggestion of the tremendous blow that the ball is about to receive.

Eye on the Ball.—Some people may argue that keeping the eye on the ball throughout the stroke is all that is necessary for accurate hitting. That may be so. But a first-class player must do more than hit accurately—he must hit hard and to a definite place. True, he must look at the ball, and at one small part of it, for that narrows the field of vision and so helps concentration, but that alone will not suffice.

One idea, as every teacher knows, can give rise to many others, so that if a central idea be carefully chosen it can in itself become the inspiration of quite an extended plan of action. If, therefore, in the address the player thinks of the need for the left side to be braced at impact, it will make him drive well, for it will lead to concentration on the essential part of the stroke.

Stoutly-built Players.—It may be well to conclude this chapter with a special word of advice to those thick-set or stout players who, for physical reasons, find it difficult to follow the advice for carrying out the details of the golf swing suggested in the two previous chapters. These suggestions had in mind, of course, the player of average build. A stoutly-built man cannot pivot so well as a slim man, but generally he is more strongly developed as regards his body, arms and wrists. He needs only to adapt his method of play somewhat to enable him to hit as far as his more slightly-built fellow, while generally his style is in the direction of greater control.

The following adaptations are suggested :—

Stance—square, with ball central between the feet.

Grip—hands farther out from the body.

Club—flatter lie.

Back-swing—round the body, without a see-saw movement of the shoulders.

Down-swing—to get a slight pull on the ball (*see* Chapter X).

57

CHAPTER VII

OTHER WOODEN CLUBS

A.—BRASSIE

The Club.—As the club is used for shots through the green a greater degree of accuracy is required for the brassie than for the driver. On the tee the ball has an inviting lie and the stance is level; usually, too, there is a wide expanse to aim at. Through the green, however, the conditions are seldom as favorable. The ball may be lying quite close, and the stance may be somewhat awkward; moreover it may be necessary to control the run on the ball after gauging the length of flight—that is, to play a highly controlled shot. For all these reasons a great measure of control of the club is required and the club must be adapted to the conditions.

First of all there should be a fair amount of loft on the club face to get the ball up. This may mean slight loss of length, but it ensures increased control; besides, it is dispiriting, especially to weak players who cannot hit hard, to find that a quite accurately played shot fails to rise.

Unless the player be a very hard hitter, the shaft should have a fair amount of whippiness, for in all specially accurate shots it is desirable to feel the club-head. It should not be quite so whippy as the driver, for the stroke is more of a hit than the drive. It is sometimes pointed out that the impact with the ground may deflect the club-head if the shaft be at all whippy, but it is doubtful whether this often happens. Certain it is that many players fail to brassie as well as they drive entirely through the stiff-shafted club having a different feel.

The shaft should be about an inch shorter than that of the driver; this ensures greater control in the swing. The lie should be fairly upright so as to enable the player to stand nearer the ball, for this, again, is in the direction of greater accuracy. The weight of the driver and brassie should be the same.

Many players use their brassie off the tee, and there is nothing to be said against this practice so long as it is not the same club that they propose to use through the green. It may be a childish thing to admit, but it is a fact, that even the most experienced players feel a certain amount of uneasiness and uncertainty when they endeavor to use a club with accuracy and restraint through the green, after swinging it with abandon on the tee. The use of a second brassie for this purpose will give better results. Faith goes a long way in golf.

59

Variations from the Driver Swing.—The swing on the tee with the driver is full and rhythmic, for the conditions are ideal. The ball is teed, the stance level, and there are no tricks to be played. The player's mind is composed. Through the green, however, circumstances are seldom so favorable. The close-lying ball will not admit of so flat a swing, which must perforce be more upright and curtailed. This means that the blow is a more descending stroke, necessitating either a very powerful swing or loft on the club. In any case the ball is taken on the downswing.

As the back-swing is upright and curtailed, an open stance becomes possible. This is really desirable, for it favors a good follow through, and this is essential to get length. The pivot, too, is more curtailed, so that there is more weight on the left foot both in the address and at the top of the swing than there was on the tee.

Although the grip is the same there should be a greater feeling of tenseness both in the grip of the left and in the left shoulder top. Indeed the whole body should be more a-quiver. The ball has to be sent almost as far as from the tee, and it has to be done with a back-swing that is both curtailed and upright. The conditions are against this being done, so that a greater effort is required by the muscles of the loins, forearms and wrists. In a word, a degree of suppleness goes out of the stroke and there should be very

60

little in the body. How often do we notice that the stiff forearm driver is also a good brassie player through his style being so well adapted to the brassie stroke.

So far we have assumed that the brassie lie is a very close one, demanding great accuracy in the stroke. It is a further step towards accuracy and control if the feet be placed nearer together, for this throws more work on the wrists and tends to cut the body twist out. In fact, it may be said here, in anticipation of what is said more fully in Chapter X, that all controlled shots, such as slices and pulls, are made with curtailed swings and taut arm muscles. Thus the wrists and loin muscles have more to do at the moment of impact, and it is essential that the player should have a very keen sense of the position of the club-head. More especially is this so if the ball is cupped, for the club-head must come down and must, at the moment of impact, be driven through and out by the wrists. Timing is absolutely essential in such shots.

We may summarize the foregoing by saying that the closer the lie the more open should be the stance and the more upright the swing.

B.—THE SPOON

The Club.—The spoon differs essentially from a brassie in having a shallower and more lofted face. Virtually it is a wooden cleek and may be used as an alternative to that club.

61

The characteristics of the head make this club ideal for playing from a very close lie, or in any situation where it is difficult to get the ball up. Being shallow in the face, the weight is concentrated immediately behind the point of impact so that a close lying ball can be driven with greater force than is possible with the brassie in the same circumstances. Of course, if the ball be sitting up well a spoon may get too far beneath it and the brassie may be preferable.

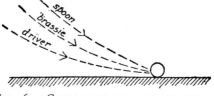

FIG. 69.—COMPARISON OF DOWN-SWING OF THE WOODEN CLUBS.

Brassie versus Spoon.—For weak players who cannot hit reasonably hard the spoon is decidedly the more useful club. It gets the ball up in situations where this would be impossible with the brassie for any one but a hard hitter. Also, as it is slightly shorter in the shaft than the brassie a great variety of spared and controlled shots can be played with it. In winter or in wet weather it is less apt to drive the ball into the turf, while in a wind the swing is more under control.

Spoon versus Cleek.—The cleek has a shorter shaft than the spoon and is more adapted for play in a high wind. But, for slicing and pulling,

62

the spoon is preferable as the ball appears to remain longer in contact with the club-head and so the desired effect can be produced. The spoon is also to be preferred to a cleek when the ball is cupped. This arises from the fact that the blow with the cleek must be a descending one, taking turf. With the spoon, however, turf is not taken because the flat sole prevents it.

FIG. 69A.—SPOON SHOT. THE CLUB-HEAD SKIDS FORWARD AFTER IMPACT WITH THE GROUND AT A.

Another point in favor of the spoon is its adaptability for playing a cut up shot. In this shot the ball is struck below the center by the ascending club-face, and one method of doing this is to bang the club-head flat on the ground behind the ball. From this it skids forwards and upwards (Fig. 69a). In similar circumstances the blade of the cleek would take turf.

Method of Play.—The stance, grip and method of executing the strokes do not differ from those required for the brassie, but the shorter shaft, heavier head, greater loft and more upright lie seem to mark the club out for very exact work. Every player ought to endeavor to master the spoon, for it is often a reliable stand-by when every other club is in disfavor (*see* Chap. VIII and Fig. 70).

63

CHAPTER VIII

FOR ADVANCED PLAYERS

HAVING dealt in considerable detail with the elements of the swing with the wooden clubs, it remains to introduce two other points which have been deliberately omitted hitherto.

These have been disregarded solely because, as every teacher knows, it is important to get the fundamentals of the swing right and, as far as possible, to get certain essentials of it out of the conscious stage and into the mechanical, before introducing any disturbing qualifications.

The two points that are now brought forward are of the utmost importance. They are equally applicable to play with the irons. They are:

1. The ball should be hit a descending blow.

2. At impact the ball should be "squeezed" or "pinched."

It will be necessary and perhaps useful first of all to recapitulate and compare some of the more salient differences in the swings of the driver, brassie and spoon, so that the reader may get a comprehensive view of what may perhaps be termed the underlying principle of wooden club play.

64

Address, &c.	Driver.	Brassie.	Spoon.
Stance	Behind and nearly square.	Slightly more advanced and more open.	More advanced and more open still.
Weight in Stance	Largely on right.	More evenly distributed.	Equally divided.
Back-Swing	Flat and Full.	More upright and shorter.	More upright and shorter still.
Weight at top.	Largely on right.	Equally distributed.	More on left.
Down-Swing	Fig. 69	Fig. 69	Fig. 69.

From this summary it should appear that whereas the driver swing is full and free, the swings with the other clubs are curtailed, and must therefore entail more rigidity of arm and wrist.

A little reflection will show that this difference in the nature of the brassie and spoon swings from that of the driver has arisen entirely from the need to deliver in their case a more descending blow, as the ball is not only not teed but may actually be lying badly. This naturally shortens the back-swing; it also hampers the follow through, so that in the jerk shot with the spoon—which may be taken as the extreme case—there is scarcely any follow through at all.

All experienced golfers who have learnt the art of playing wristy shots out of unfavorable lies will know that the main concern in such

65

cases is not to get the ball up but so to manipu-
late the club-head that the ball flies straight,
and not out to the right as it is apt to do. There
arises in consequence, in the minds of many
players, the idea that this method of playing the
brassie and spoon is not inherently good but is
merely the best thing to do in the unfortunate
situation forced upon them.

Now what it is desired to point out here is
that this descending blow necessitates a movement of the forearms and wrists which is really
of the very essence and soul of golf, and should
really be brought into the tee shot as well. This
action is usually termed "pinching" or "squeezing," and may briefly be described in connection
with Figs. 71 and 72.

FIG. 71.—CLUB-FACE SHUT AT IMPACT—HANDS
AHEAD OF THE CLUB-HEAD.

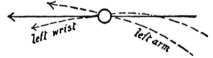

FIG. 72.—PLAN SHOWING ACTION OF LEFT
ARM AND WRIST IN THE "SQUEEZING"
STROKE.

Fig. 72 is a ground-plan showing the ball
and the line of flight; Fig. 71 is a section of the
same. If the ball be played in the direction

66

shown, it is obvious that it will not fly straight, but will be outside the line to the hole. This must be prevented by playing the ball with the club-face shut, as shown in Fig. 71. When the head reaches the lowest point in the downward arc, the club-face is opened. All this is done by the left wrist, while the right comes in only at the finish when the face has opened. The right is the stronger wrist, but care must be taken not to attempt this movement with the right wrist. There is a natural tendency to forget the left wrist in all golf shots, and if, in this stroke, the mind dwells on the right, the left is apt to be cut out of the stroke and so fail to fulfill its proper function of guiding and also, in this case, of turning the club-face.

Finally, it must be observed that the hands should be ahead of the club-head until the club-face is opened. If they are behind, it will be impossible to prevent pulling if the face be shut, and slicing if it be open.

It is obvious that in the down-swing the player should be keenly aware of the position of the club-head. He must not attempt this finish to the stroke until his hip pivot and swing have become mechanical, for not until then is he free in the down-swing to concentrate on this final work of the wrists.

To summarize, then, the player must:

1. Play down.

67

2. Keep the hands ahead of the club-head until the ball is struck.

3. Shut the club-face at impact by means of the left wrist.

On reconsidering this advice one feels that it may be argued that it all points to an attempt to make the player use his wrists. Undoubtedly that is so, for he will get length and he will get control. And the only way in which he can get this maximum value out of his wrist work, without slicing or pulling violently, is by hitting down with a shut face.

CHAPTER IX

THE DRIVE—LENGTH

As the club is gripped by the hands, and these, in turn, swung by the arms, there is a tendency vastly to overrate the part played by the arms and wrists in the golf swing. This is perhaps only natural, when we consider how constantly we are using these parts of the body to help us through life, and how sensitively they are attuned to the nerve centers of the brain.

But a golf swing by the medium of an arm and wrist movement alone is a feeble thing; it is only necessary to sit on a table and swing a club to realize this fully. Something more is required than merely arm movement.

Let us consider for a moment what can be done by keeping the arms still and rigid and making a see-saw movement of the shoulders. Quite a long ball can be hit in this way. If we give this last exercise a little thought we realize that the legs are playing an important part in it; that, in fact, it is dependent very largely on a good foothold and on bending at the knees. We could not hit the ball far if the stance were on ice.

Now let us consider what happens if we keep the arms rigid and try to drive the ball by

69

pivoting at the hips. Wherein lies the motive power in this case? Clearly again the legs come into this movement, even more than in the see-saw movement. That is the first discovery. But what are the conditions for getting the shoulders back in the return movement? There appear to be two. First the back muscles must keep a rigid connection between the left shoulder and the right hip; and secondly the right leg and side must be braced and holding, so that when the time for the return swing has come the whole of the trunk above the hip can be moved by *unwinding the right thigh and so causing what may be called a hip-swing.*

This movement loses power if the muscles from the hip are not braced, for the hips would rotate under the shoulders, leaving them behind. The player must make the down stroke now by means of the arms and wrists only—like the player sitting on the table.

Let us now consider the case where the back muscles are braced but when there is no pivoting. The stroke is performed by the arm muscles acting from a rigid center, viz., the left shoulder. The chip and putt are cases of this kind. There is a stern limit to the length that can be obtained. Why? Because there is no pivot and the left shoulder is held.

In driving, then, there are two things to be controlled, viz., the arms and wrists, and the trunk to which the arms are attached.

70

Practice Hints.—Throughout this book the player is advised to get width in his back-swing; that is, to fling his hands as far along the line of flight as possible, for this will bring the shoulders round and so necessitate a full pivot.

If at the very outset of his practice he attempts to get width, he will be apt to overswing; that is, the upper part of his body will screw in excess of the power of the hips to control it.

Clearly then the correct way to proceed is to forget the arms above and think only of the hips beneath until a full, braced hip-pivot becomes mechanical. The player should now feel that he can play the down-swing from his loins and that he has prepared his body beforehand by a backward sway and a braced turn of the hips.

When he can thus move freely "beneath himself" (Figs. 20, 28) he can proceed with advantage to lengthen out the back-swing, for the body is prepared to resist the torsion. The swing is now founded on a rock-like base adjusted and braced for the purpose.

Length.—If the player has had control of his poise in the back-swing so that he can sling his hips freely and strongly in the down-swing, great power will be felt.

Length is not got by extra arm or wrist movement; such attempts usually result in over swinging or loss of rhythm.

The secret lies in manipulation of the hips and in extra rigidity of the left side at impact. The arms, through the hips, are brought down with great speed and power on to the ball, and if they are also braced, the wrists have then little more to do than to firm up and sustain the blow at impact. For the blow partakes then of the nature of the boxer's punch, being both fast and sustained.

Hard hitting, as a first-class player understands it, is not pressing: there is little in the nature of extra wrist work in it, and certainly there is a scarcely perceptible increase in the pivot. Whenever extra length is required the trunk and leg muscles are specially braced, they are all a-quiver and specially under control in the address. When the swing commences the pivot is already mapped out in the mind, the appropriate muscles are on guard and a special hip and body effort is easy to accomplish.

To cultivate length, then, it is necessary to strengthen the muscles from the knee to the neck, but above all, to have them responsive to the will. A player must not be muscle-bound; his muscles must possess flexibility.

Control then of these muscles must be acquired by practice, by pivot practice, for this in addition will improve the player's sense of balance and lead to concerted action; in a word, to good timing.

CHAPTER X

SLICING AND PULLING—THE SLICE

The Shot.—Most golfers have served a long, unwilling apprenticeship to the art of slicing, and are already familiar with some of the conditions that favor the making of the stroke. In this chapter an endeavor is made to show them some of the things they have been doing, and must do, if they wish to make the shot at will.

Of all advanced shots the slice is the easiest to make. This arises partly from the fact that as the player stands very open, with the obstacle to be circumvented right in front of him, he has little difficulty in framing a clear mental picture of the object to be achieved. But slicing comes specially easy to most of us through the natural tendency to pull the arms in towards the body at impact and so cut across the ball. It was pointed out earlier, in the chapter on the Downswing, that the hands should return as near to the body as possible and not outwards, so that at impact they may be able to travel forward parallel to the line of flight. Naturally, if we wish to slice, this downward movement of the hands should, at first, be outwards, so that at

73

impact they are beginning to come inwards across the line of flight.

The Task.—Suppose the ball to be at A (Fig. 73), and it is required to slice round a belt of trees at B in order to reach the green at C, which is well within range. Clearly the straight

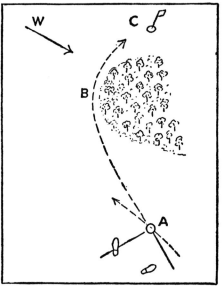

FIG. 73.—STANCE FOR SLICING ROUND AN
OBSTACLE.

line from A to C is not the line of flight, and so must be cut out of the discussion. The real line is as shown, viz., A B, and that is the line of flight referred to below. It must be mapped out by the player in the address and the stance must be taken up with reference to it.

Having settled on the line of flight he must next determine in his own mind the amount of

74

slice required, what deviation there must be in the air, and what on the ground. If the shot is with wood, and is therefore of considerable length, the amount of spin required will be less than for a shorter shot with, say, an iron, for there is more space in which the slice can develop.

The wind, too, has to be taken into account. If, for example, it be from the quarter shown by the arrow W, little, if any, slice will be necessary, for the wind will give part or all of the bias required.

The Club.—It is pointed out below that the face of the club must be open at impact, and must continue open during impact. This obviously demands a straight-faced club, that is, a face with little loft; thus a driver is preferable to a brassie, an iron to a mashie, and so on. This is further advisable from the fact that the swing for the slice is curtailed and the nature of the blow delivered is all against length. The tendency in slicing is to be short, therefore it is a wise thing to over-club. And above all things the player must have courage.

THE ADDRESS AND SWING

Grip.—Left hand on side facing the hole, one knuckle showing.

Right hand on top.

This grip is important as it enables the player to keep the club-face open.

75

Stance.—Very open, with ball, roughly, opposite left toe—feet usual distance apart for that club (Fig. 74).

Club-face.—Laid back.

Back-Swing.—Bring the club back outside the line of flight, keeping the right elbow well into the side. The pivot must be restricted, so that the shoulders make a see-saw movement. The back-swing must have width.

Down-Swing.—By means of the left, return the club-head along A C reversed and hit under and inwards as if it were a mashie shot, the club-face being kept open.

NOTES

1.—To keep the club-face open during impact, and while cutting across the ball, the hands must finish in front of the body. This necessitates the left hip being brought well out of the way and so accounts for the very open stance. It is a principle to be observed right throughout the gamut of golfing strokes that care should be taken both in the address and in the back-swing not to do anything that will interfere with the easy and correct return of the club. Now, many failures to progress are directly traceable to a breach of this principle. One of the commonest examples is a circular sweep round the body; for the left hip is brought so far round, too, that it cannot be got out of the way again in the down-swing. Loss of length is the usual

76

result; so if length is desired keep off the heels in the back-swing.

2.—The right elbow must not leave the side in the back-swing, otherwise the right hand will take control and lift. Loss of width results.

3.—A curtailed swing throws more work upon the wrists; which is highly desirable in this shot. The sweep across the ball and the keeping open of the club-face are the work of the wrists, and any attempt to lessen their responsibility, as by a large pivot, is apt to lead to disaster. Hence in the address and throughout the stroke the concentration should be on the wrists and the club-head, and the body-movement should be automatic. Not until this automatic stage is reached ought the player to attempt slices in important contests.

4.—It is desirable to get a wide swing without lifting the hands very high and this cannot be done by a snatchy, hurried back-swing. Slowness and calmness should characterize the stroke, for the feeling of calm composure will not only encourage a wide back-swing but will help to time the wrist action correctly.

THE PULL

The Shot.—This shot is the reverse of a slice. At impact the club-head is describing an arc which is passing outwards across the line of flight, thus imparting a right to left spin. Both

77

physically and mentally the stroke is more difficult to bring off than a slice; physically, because the arms must go out from the body, at and after impact, and this requires a distinct physical effort; mentally, because the player, through his stance, has an unusual difficulty in visualizing the proper path the ball has to take.

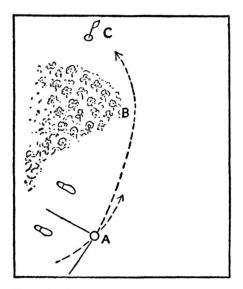

FIG. 76.—STANCE FOR PULLING ROUND AN OBSTACLE.

The Task.—Suppose the ball to be at A (Fig. 76), and a belt of trees at B shuts off the green. A pulled shot to escape the trees should take the path A B C as shown. In this case the line of flight is indicated by the line A B and the stance must be taken up relative to A B.

The dotted arrow indicates the direction of

78

the club-head at impact; it will be seen to cut the line of flight from within outwards.

The Club.—The success of the stroke requires the wrists and forearms to be rolled over at impact and during contact. For this purpose a lofted club is best, for a straight-faced club would drive the ball down. Thus a cleek is preferable to an iron, a brassie to a driver, and so on. A good spoon is invaluable for this purpose.

Also, it is advisable to over-club oneself as the tendency is to be short. If there be doubt about getting the length when it is proposed to pull or slice, it would be much wiser to play for safety by a straight-forward shot to the flank of the trees and a chip, or what not, to the green. The pull must not finish among the trees: and the risk must be well weighed up. Many golfers thrive on difficulties and play their best shots when the occasion specially demands them; the necessity for a pull or a slice acts as a tonic to such people, and the vim and zest with which they tackle it assures success at the outset. There are others, however, who see only the horrid consequences of failure, and quail even as they take up their stance.

THE ADDRESS AND SWING

Grip.—Left hand slightly on top of shaft—about three knuckles showing.

Right hand slightly under the shaft.

79

This grip enables the player more easily to shut the club-face during impact.

Stance.—Very slightly open—almost square, with the ball midway between the feet (Fig. 75).

Back-swing.—By means of the left hand, and with both elbows tucked in, fling the club in a wide sweep round the body, keeping the face shut as long as possible.

Down-swing.—1.—Bring the hands downwards as near the body as possible and fling them outwards at impact so as to send the club-head across the ball.

2.—At impact roll the wrists and forearms over so as to shut the club-face.

NOTES

1.—In the back-swing avoid the tendency to swing the club at once round the body, or else the shot will be ruined. Keep the left elbow well in and get width and so keep the weight at top on the right toe. If the sweeping movement begins at once, the left hip comes round and cannot be got out of the way in the down-swing. The fling away, rather than round, induces a smaller left hip movement, and as the position at top is more open there is more time in the down-swing to get that hip away and fling through and after the ball.

2.—The turning over of the wrists and forearms to shut the face needs accurate timing and

80

gauging. This means that the mind must concentrate from the beginning on this wrist movement and must not for a moment lose touch with the club-head.

3.—Swing slowly, especially in the backswing; any extra effort at this point cannot fail to weaken the concentration and upset the timing. In this stroke, more perhaps than in any other, the behavior of the club-head after impact is of tremendous importance and the effort should be delayed as late as possible.

4.—Above all things visualize throughout the stroke the part you wish the club-head to play.

CHAPTER XI

PLAY IN THE WIND

Introductory.—If a man wishes to know how to play in a wind the best advice one can give him is "Go out into it and learn." And when he has learned how to use it as an ally and to cheat it as an enemy he will have learnt many valuable things. He will have learnt, for example, how to pull and how to slice, how to cut a ball up and how to keep it down, and above all, he will have learnt the most valuable thing of all, namely, how to take up a stance, use his feet, and keep his balance. Fortunate is the golfer who has served his apprenticeship by the seaside, for he has learnt so much that others can seldom teach him.

This chapter, therefore, is not intended for him, but for that large majority who have not had his advantages, and to whom a game in the wind is as rare as it is distressing.

Two observations on the detailed advice appear to be necessary at this point, for they may help to create the right mental background. First, that it is as necessary to take such precautions as will help the player to maintain his balance as it is to control the ball. Loss of balance will usually have a greater effect on the result of his stroke than the play of the wind on the ball.

Secondly, that as the body throughout the stroke is naturally at an abnormal state of tension, a free swing is not physically possible, and the modifications suggested have this fact in mind.

Down-wind.—1. Stand slightly more open and keep the club-face open: this will tend to get the ball up (Fig. 77).

2. Stand further behind the ball to allow for the wind moving the body slightly forward in the down-swing.

3. Curtail the back-swing a little—or lock earlier.

4. From the top onwards fight with the left side to keep the body back and so maintain the timing.

5. Concentrate on the club-head, and this will keep the left hip in the right position; a braced left hip is required to help to resist the force of the wind.

6. A see-saw movement of the shoulders rather than a free pivot is advisable in order to keep a good balance at the top and, further, to ensure a firm left hip.

Against-wind.—1. Stand slightly more square than the normal stance, and with the ball slightly in rear of left heel (Fig. 78).

2. Take a shorter grip.

3. Keep the left elbow well in, so as to shut

83

the club-face, and see that the back-swing is well beneath the body. This means that the left shoulder has dipped rather than turned and that at the top the weight is, if anything, more on the left foot than the right.

4. Swing slowly back.

5. Any attempt to keep the club-face shut after impact may meet with disaster, as the wrist movement is difficult to time.

6. Think of the club-head and remember that it should strike a descending blow.

Cross-wind.—The simplest cases of a cross-wind are shown in Figs. 79 and 80. The natural inclination of the inexperienced player is to play straight into it, in the hope that the ball will be blown back onto the fairway. This is about the worst policy to adopt; length is lost in the

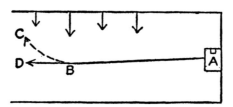

FIG. 79.—SLICING INTO THE WIND.

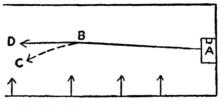

FIG. 80.—PULLING INTO THE WIND.

84

battle against the wind and the spent ball may be driven anywhere. Besides, the enemy will mercilessly emphasize any pull or slice that has been inadvertently imparted.

The proper course to adopt is shown in Figs. 79 and 80. It will be seen that in each case use has actually been made of the wind by driving slightly towards that side of the fairway to which it is blowing. In the section AB of its flight, the wind is an ally. At point B the effect of the pull or slice begins to work, so that the ball is now tending to fly against the wind. The result is that instead of deviating along the dotted path BC, it continues along the line BD.

Of course, the wind may blow at a different angle from that shown, but the principle suggested above still holds good. If the wind be more at the player's back, he will drive straighter and with less pull or slice; if more against him, he will impart more bias.

Chapter XII

THE IRON CLUBS

General Note.—All the iron clubs—iron, mashie, etc.—are designed for use chiefly when a controlled shot is required. Generally speaking, the shot to the green is a controlled shot; the aim is to hit the ball to a certain spot in such a way that its subsequent run will take it to the green. For this purpose one of the iron clubs is usually employed, the choice being determined largely by the distance to be covered and by the nature of the immediate approach.

For quite short distances the mashie or mashie-niblick would be employed, as their short shafts and set-back faces tend to great accuracy. For longer shots one of the irons would be used. Whatever club is used, the main object to be attained is exact length.

Now ability to achieve a certain definite length involves ability to do two things: to control the length of flight, and to control the subsequent run. When the player can do both of these things he may be said to have mastered the most difficult shot in golf. Control of run is not a difficult matter. In the case of the mashie and mashie-niblick, the loft of the club will of itself

86

impart, as a rule, the necessary control after the ball has pitched, and the beginner, at any rate, would be well advised to leave that task to the club. If additional control is required, then one of the more advanced shots dealt with in Chapter XVI should be employed. In any case it is the way in which the ball is hit that determines the amount of run, and the necessary skill to do this is not difficult to acquire. It is, however, the fault of very many players that they concentrate too early in their golfing career on control of run instead of mastering first of all control of flight. For control of run depends, no matter what device is adopted, on the manner of playing the down-stroke. On the other hand, control of length of flight depends mainly on the back-swing. It is obvious, then, that control of flight should be mastered first; it would be putting the cart before the horse to proceed otherwise.

If it be conceded that the professional player is superior to the amateur, the disparity would appear to be most marked in the shot to the pin. The professional gauges the length of flight better, and this would at once imply that he has a method of control which pervades all his iron club play. What that method is will be explained in the following chapters, for it is one of the secrets of success with the iron clubs.

Full Shots.—So far, stress has been laid on the need for control of length in playing an iron club. But it may be argued that most players

87

make full shots with their irons, habitually using the club solely to get length. This is undoubtedly true. The short shaft, thin sole and encouraging loft of the iron clubs make a stronger appeal to the average player than the brassie with its longer shaft, straight face and broad sole. Further, if the ball is lying close, the player fears a foozle with the brassie with its comparatively flat swing and plumps for the iron; he knows that he can get as far with a nicely hit iron as with a semi-foozled brassie and the shot will give him greater pleasure. Some players are in the habit of hitting prodigious distances with their irons and if they carry a brassie at all seldom use it. Such players may be termed "full shot" players, for instead of attempting half-irons they play full shots with mashie or mashie-niblick. This habit of full swinging is responsible for much lack of progress, for the player does not learn ball control.

In the Hints on Practice in Chapter I, players were specially urged to commence with short controlled shots with all the iron clubs, in the hope that their attitude towards these clubs should be first and foremost not length but control of length.

CHOICE OF CLUBS

At least two irons should be included in every one's set, viz., a No. 1 iron and a No. 2, or mid-iron.

88

The mid-iron should have a medium deep face and should be as deep at the heel as at the toe. It should be lighter than the No. 1 iron. This iron will be used for the shorter shots and is useful for run up approaches.

The No. 1 iron is for heavier and longer work. A cleek is really preferable to a No. 1 iron; not the old-fashioned straight faced club which so often took the place of the brassie in the old gutty days, but the modern cleek with a lofted face. There are two reasons for preferring the cleek: first, the ball promises to get up more quickly and so begets confidence, and secondly, the face being shallower, the weight is more concentrated behind the point of impact. Thus the cleek has more driving power. The cleek, like the iron, should be as deep at the heel as at the toe.

These two clubs should be in every bag. In addition to these, however, it is advisable under certain conditions to include also a jigger or No. 3 iron.

The jigger resembles a cleek in appearance but is shorter in the shaft and has the weight of a mid-iron. It is more useful than the mid-iron when the fairway is wet and heavy and the ball is lying close.

A mashie and mashie-niblick would complete the set.

The mashie should not be light nor should it have too much loft. In playing certain strokes it is necessary to shut the face and in playing others to open it; thus a medium loft is best. A good blade has as much loft at the heel as at the toe, but it is to be feared that this is a point that some makers do not sufficiently recognize.

The mashie-niblick should have the characteristics of the mashie except that the blade has, of course, more loft. Both clubs should have deep blades.

Shafts.—The shafts of all irons should have a fair amount of spring in them. In addition to inducing the hands to move over and under the grip and so shut the face, stiff shafts are apt to lead to bad timing; for the player is less conscious of the weight of the club-head and, in consequence, it is not allowed to do its full share of the work.

It may be objected that if a heavy divot be taken the springy shaft might twist when the stiff shaft would not, but the fault in that case does not lie with the club. Properly played, the iron head should brush the grass without taking a large divot. The mashie and mashie-niblick should have stronger shafts than the iron.

The shaft of the iron should be only slightly longer than that of the mashie: a short shaft tends to accuracy. Besides, in short run-ups with the iron the shorter shaft is less likely to get entangled with the dress. There is also the further advantage that with short shafted irons there is less bending of the wrists at the top and, as is pointed out later, this is a very important matter in playing an iron.

90

Chapter XIII

THE IRON—BACK-SWING

A.—Preliminaries

(Figs. 86-97)

Stance.—Slightly more open than for the driver or brassie. This is because the swing will be more upright and the pivot restricted.

Weight.—There is slightly more weight on the left than there was in the drive, but all the same the weight should be behind the ball. It may be stated here that from the drive right down to the mashie-niblick the nearer stance has a tendency to throw the weight more and more from the right foot to the left at the top of the swing. In any case there is never more on the left than on the right in the address except in the case of a short pitch with the mashie or mashie-niblick. To summarize the advice: "For length keep the weight on the right, for short shots keep it more and more on the left."

Address.—Ground the club with the shaft slightly in advance of the club-head, so that the grip is in line with the ball. A shaft bent by use should not be discarded unless, of course, the spring is entirely gone. Such clubs are really very valuable in that the hands in the address are ahead of the blade.

Stand so that the club can be gripped with the left arm hanging fully extended in front of the body. The shaft should be as nearly horizontal as possible and the toe of the club should be practically off the ground. Keep the left shoulder up and the left arm taut. The grip with the left should be firm. The right hand should be well over the shaft. The left shoulder should be braced, for this brings the hands forward and so tempts the player to get width.

Both elbows should be in and the right elbow should be pointing to the ground. The player should be almost looking down at the top of the ball, and not at the inner side as when driving. The ball should be opposite the left heel.

B.—THE BACK-SWING
INSTRUCTIONS

1. A slight forward and downward movement of the right hip, causing the hands to move slightly forward.

2. A lateral and upward movement of the right hip to the right, parallel to the line of flight. Brace the right leg from the knee downward.

3. At the same time the hands will come back, bringing the club-head backwards along the line of flight and the left will then lift until stopped by the left shoulder.

NOTES

There are certain details in connection with these movements that are extremely important, for it is in the making of the back-swing that length of flight is controlled.

1. The backward movement of the hands should be well under the body. (Figs. 23-28.)

2. The hands should not sweep up round the body (Figs. 81, 82), otherwise the player will be tied up at the top: he will not be able to get back.

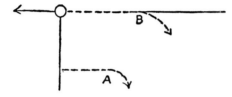

FIG. 81.—CORRECT BACK-SWING. THE HANDS SHOULD GO BACK TO A AND THE CLUB-HEAD TO B BEFORE BEING CONSCIOUSLY LIFTED.

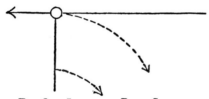

FIG. 82.—INCORRECT BACK-SWING.

His left hip will come round too much and his left shoulder not enough. In the back-swing, while the club-head is being dragged along the line of flight, and before the left hand begins the lifting movement, both elbows should be moving along as nearly as possible in contact with the body and should only leave it when the club-

93

head is rising to its place over the shoulder. This lifting movement begins with the pivot; that is, after the hip swing and not before.

3. Keep both elbows as near together as possible throughout: this will have the effect of keeping the left arm straight and thus of bringing the left shoulder round; further, the right hand will be less likely to interfere in this part of the swing. When the right elbow sticks out away from the side the backward swing by the left hand has been lost sight of and the right hand is doing the work.

4. When the player has braced the right leg from the knee downwards, the backward sweep of the hands has the effect of turning or twisting the right leg from the knee to the hip. When the twist has proceeded far enough (in the player's judgment) he will stop the rotation and brace the muscles of the back. This will have the effect of stopping the backward movement of the left shoulder. A great strain is put at this point on the muscles on the inner side of the right thigh. But the whole point of this matter lies in the fact that the extent to which the left shoulder can follow the arms in the back-swing depends on the extent to which the right thigh has twisted and on the bracing of the muscles across the back to the left shoulder top.

5. As a result of this controlled rigidity of the right side and back, the left shoulder will really appear to the player to be fighting against the

94

backward movement of the arms. And this is actually so: in fact, the resistance of the left shoulder is almost the most conscious act in the back-swing, for the point at which the left shoulder stops, coupled with the amount of tautness in the left arm, *together control the length of flight.* To the observer it would appear that the movement of the left shoulder in the pivot is a deliberate and conscious movement which has had the result of taking the arms and club back and of causing the pivot at the hips; that, in fact, the sweeping backward turn of the left shoulder is the mainspring of the back-swing. It comes as a surprise to the beginner to learn that the only conscious movement backward is that of the hands—and, of course, the lateral movement of the right hip mentioned in paragraph 2, p. 38, and that the player is actually endeavoring to twist his left shoulder towards the hole. So little can we really learn by watching.

6. The backward movement of the arms should be a leisurely movement; all the hurrying-up needed in the stroke is required at the point when the right hand comes into the down-stroke (*see* Down-swing, pp. 103, 104).

7. At the top of the swing there must be a tenseness from the top of the left shoulder along the biceps, forearm and wrist, and the grip of both hands should be firm. The hands are brought to a standstill by a jerk from the left

95

shoulder, and the club-head swings up and, as it were, compresses the wrists. This compression is needed to start the club-head in the return swing, and ability to wait for it is at once the secret of the nippiness that characterizes the good iron player.

Some players, especially elderly ones, drop the wrists when the time comes and the shaft passes on to touch the right shoulder top. Some wait for the rebound off the shoulder and so get a slight, if ungainly, compensation. But the majority have to start the club back by the wrists, which through bending have lost power and have lost time. The unpivoting starts and the rest of the stroke is a labored mis-timed heave.

8. The grip of the right hand is important, for although the right must be kept out of the back-swing so far as the slinging of the club is concerned, yet this is, as it were, a period of preparation, for the right is coming into the stroke later on.

It may be said that all the thought expended in getting the left hand moving correctly is really to get everything in readiness for the time when the right is coming in. The punch comes from the right when all is said and done, but the right by itself will not get a good length nor will it tend to accuracy of either length or direction. The left, then, controls, and the right supplies the sinews.

The right hand should be well over the shaft

96

in the address and the right elbow well in. As the hands swing back the grip of the right should not relax; at the top, and to the finish of the stroke, it should be very fierce indeed, but especially with the thumb and forefinger. This is only possible if the right elbow is kept in in the back-swing, in which case the right forearm actually rotates slightly backwards. At the top of the swing, if the player cares to look for the purposes of following these instructions, the right hand will be seen to be obscuring the left; that is, to be underneath it. The ham of the thumb will be practically covering the base knuckle of the left forefinger.

The player will find it profitable practice to swing a light iron, first with the left hand and then with the right, and note the muscular and pivotal adjustments that have separately to be made.

9. Nothing so far has been said about the left leg, and it is as well if, in the back-swing, the player forgets that he has one. But it is important that the left shoulder be kept up in the longer shots, for this will tend to a fuller pivot. If the left shoulder be dropped unduly, the stroke is apt to develop into a see-saw movement instead of a pivot, the left shoulder coming down and the right up in the back-swing, and the reverse in the down-swing. The left shoulder in the back-swing will be slightly lower than the right, but the player should endeavor to keep it up.

97

Summary.—When the player has stopped the rotation of his right thigh, his muscles should concentrate on stopping the backward movement of the left shoulder. His hands will go back till the left arm is taut. The club-head will go back till the wrists are taut. The player is now wound up like a spring. The downward blow is not going to be merely an arm movement: it is going to be delivered from the hips.

CHAPTER XIV

THE IRON—DOWN-SWING

A.

(Figs. 86-97)

Position at Top of Swing.—In the last chapter the player was left at the top of the swing. Let us for a moment reconsider the position, as we did in the case of the driver swing.

It is a situation of great tenseness. His weight is largely on the right, but there is much more on the left than in the case of the drive, and the left knee has not bent inward very much towards the right, but has bent forward towards the line of flight, the left heel being momentarily raised.

The right side is braced and the left shoulder is holding hard, fighting, as it were, against the pivot, so that there is a tautness along the left arm. The wrists have not broken, but they have been bent back momentarily by the momentum of the club-head. The passage of the left arm across the body with the elbow almost leading, not bent, has had the effect of partially shutting the club face. The eye is intent on the ball. The hands have not swept markedly round the

99

right shoulder, but have come back parallel to the line of flight.

B.

PLAYING INSTRUCTIONS

1. Pause.
2. Untwist slowly at the hips (Figs. 90-3).
3. Bring the club down with the left, keeping that arm as straight as possible, making at the same time a slightly forward movement of the right hip parallel to the line of flight.
4. When the body is square to the line of flight brace the left leg and speed up the wrists.
5. At impact, send the left arm after the ball as far as possible, so timing the stroke that the club-head strikes a descending blow and reaches the lowest point in its arc an inch in front of the ball (Fig. 83).

FIG. 83.—CORRECT IMPACT WITH IRONS—CLUB-HEAD IS DESCENDING, TAKING TURF IN FRONT OF THE BALL.

C.

NOTES ON THE INSTRUCTIONS

1. The pause is really imperceptible as such to the onlooker, but it is a definite stoppage in the player's mental process.

Whenever such a pause is not made, and this

happens often, for most people are wound up and anxious to get the business over, the result in nearly every case is a forward movement of the upper part of the body towards the hole. This not only means that the body is displaced from the correct position when the ball is dispatched, thus rendering true hitting extremely improbable, but it leads to endless mistakes.

To begin with, the anxiety to get to grips with the ball is an elemental impulse—it is implanted firmly in the character of every beginner. Also, the impulse to use the right is equally strong and equally natural. In the hurried down-stroke the unbridled golfer brings in his right and the left is forgotten. Watch such a player. His left comes down and round with a horrid bend at the elbow; the club-head, propelled and flicked by the right, comes across the ball from right to left and there is no follow through. The ball gets up and slices off into the rough.

As a matter of fact, the correct down-stroke is not a natural movement at all; it has to be acquired, and this is true whether we consider the beginning of the movement or the movement after impact.

2. The downward movement of a straight left necessitates a straight rock-like left leg. During the down-stroke the left hip, which came forward towards the ball in the pivot, must be got back again by fetching down the left heel. Do

not hurry this hip movement—do nothing hurriedly. High speed machinery has to start slowly and must be given time to gather speed. The grounding of the left heel brings up the left shoulder, which has dipped in the back-swing, and so enables the straight left to go through the ball and not dig the ground behind. Every muscle should be concentrated on keeping the left shoulder back and up, and the left arm straight. Think of this throughout the stroke; think of it in the address (p. 55).

But the return movement of a straight left is almost impossible without a preliminary pause to enable the compression of the wrists to restart the club-head. Then the biceps come into play and the task is not now so difficult, for the club-head is already moving.

The hip-twist precedes the shoulder movements (*see* p. 71, also Figs. 90-93).

The downward movement of the left arm is not downwards and outwards: the elbow should hug the body. The outwards movement takes place after impact: it was in order to allow of this "through" movement after impact that the player was advised to stand as near the ball as possible in the address. In the back-swing he was advised to play, as it were, under himself; that is, to bring his elbows back brushing his body. Similarly in the down-swing his hands must not go out along or towards the line of flight but must come down towards his knees.

The wrists, up to the moment when the body is again square with the line and the left heel is down, must not have consciously unbent: the wrist action is deferred as long as possible and can be left till this point. So far concentration has been solely on keeping the head down, the body back and the left arm straight.

3. Length of flight depends upon the speed of the club-head while in contact with the ball and upon the duration of the period of contact. Most players think chiefly of hitting the ball hard; they do not give enough thought to the advantage to be gained by hitting it for a long time.

As the club-head is coming on to the ball the player must concentrate on sending it as far as possible after the ball and in contact with it. Greatest speed of the club-head must be just

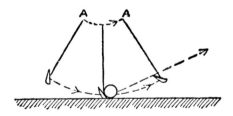

Fig. 84.—Hands (A) not flung forward—a short, lofted shot results.
Compare with Fig. 85.

after impact. The left arm must now go forward while the wrists are fetching the club-head through with great firmness. The farther forward the left can go the farther will contact with the ball be possible. At the finish of the

103

effective part of the stroke the left is fully extended.

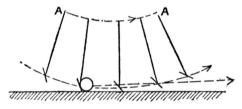

FIG. 85.—CLUB DESCRIBING A FLAT ARC
THROUGH A FORWARD FLING OF THE HANDS
FROM A TO A. THIS IS THE ESSENTIAL
ACTION OF THE PUSH SHOT.

So far nothing has been said about the right arm which, after all, is the better half in the partnership. The right will come in "on its own" all too soon: but its efforts must be properly directed. That is the function of the feebler left, for if these instructions have been followed carefully, the effort of the right will have been influenced in two main ways, viz.:

(*a*) the inward turning movement of the right as it climbs over the left will be counterbalanced by the outward motion of the left;

(*b*) the upward motion of the club-head due to the flick—which would send the ball skywards—is counteracted by the forward movement of the left, for the arc that the club-head would otherwise describe is lengthened and so contact with the ball is lengthened also. And not only so, but the flatter arc keeps the ball down and imparts desirable back spin (Figs. 84, 85, also p. 46).

104

4. At impact the wrists must be very firm and the grip tight. The flick referred to above is not entirely a wrist movement but is partly a rolling towards the hole of the forearms.

Good timing really means putting in this speeding up movement in such a way and at such a moment that it is exactly corrected by the action of the left.

If you watch a first-class iron player it will be noticed that his left leg is firm and that, at impact and after, his right shoulder comes down and through. This down and forward action of the right shoulder is puzzling to most people, but it is inevitable if the right hand is to follow the left through the ball. Of course, if the left leg did not keep firm the right shoulder would not need to dip so much, but in that case the left hand would go partially out of action.

5. Probably the most characteristic symptom of a weak player is a chronic slice. Experience has proved to him that if he whips over his right or uses it at all a horrid pull results, and he avoids this because he knows how to avoid it. Thus his right hand goes out of the shot almost entirely, and he remains a feeble slicer to the end of his days. The remedy lies in a straight left, for then the pull-effect of the whip over will be neutralized. The ensuing ball in that case should not only be free from either pull or slice, if the timing be right, but should be soul-satisfying as well.

6. As the iron and mashie are fairly short in the shaft, they can be swung quite easily with one hand. Every player ought at least to practice swinging a club with the left hand or, better still, he should play a ball. Conviction of the truth of the advice given in this chapter would soon follow. The proper way to use the left hand and arm would soon be learnt, and it is perhaps the surest way of learning to keep the left leg firm and the body back. The action resembles that of a left-handed tennis player playing a backhanded stroke.

Similar practice with the right hand should follow. In this practice care should be taken to stiffen the right leg in the back-swing and to keep the elbow near the body as long as possible. In all these practices the ball should be played.

D.

FULL MASHIE

The method of playing a full mashie shot would be exactly the same as for playing the full iron, but the player is strongly dissuaded from so using the club. Whenever such a length presents itself a spared shot with the iron should be attempted.

A half or three-quarter swing should be the limit for a mashie. In this case the right hand should not creep over the left after impact. The face of the club will thus point to the hole. Direction is best secured by this method.

106

FINAL HINTS ON IRON CLUB PLAY

1. *Hang on firmly throughout with the fore part of the grip of both hands.*
2. *Keep the hands down in the address.*
3. *Push the club under and up in the back-swing.*
4. *Try to keep the swing of the hands parallel to the line of flight throughout. This will enable you to hit down and so with power.*
5. *Don't swing the arms round your body, for the return swing will lack power.*
6. *Let the swing back with the left be resisted by the right hip.*
7. *See-saw with the shoulders as much as possible in the shorter shots, for this will help your hands to go back and return correctly.*
8. *Get the right shoulder as high as possible at the top of the swing as the right arm cannot hit down from a low position.*
9. *Don't allow a turning movement of the left shoulder until the right hip has locked and the hands begin consciously to lift.*
10. *Get the feeling that the club-head has not left the line of flight and that at the beginning of the back-swing it travels outside it.*
11. *Hit down and through the ball.*
12. *Keep the club-face slightly shut at impact.*

107

Chapter XV

SHORT APPROACHES—THE PITCH-AND-RUN

(Figs. 99-101)

A.—Introductory

So far we have dealt only with wooden clubs and irons and our chief concern has been to get the correct hip swing going, and to help the player in other ways so that he might get his long shot away far and straight. We have been dealing, then, mainly with the problem of length. True, in the chapters on the iron, our thoughts have been divided between the acquisition of length and its control, and the player has been repeatedly advised not to go all out with irons, but to endeavor to secure control, yet the instructions had in view the object mainly of enabling the player to get length from a controlled swing.

But now we put length behind us, as it were, and propose in this chapter and the next to discuss the various ways of playing the approach. At the outset it may be said that in the instructions about to be given we are not concerned with the question of getting length but almost solely with that of controlling the run. Control of run near the green is almost everything; lacking that the excellence of the rest of one's game counts almost as nothing.

Now in the question of control of length two aspects of each shot have separately and jointly to be considered, namely, length of flight and length of run. That is to say when an approach shot confronts him the player has to decide how far the ball shall fly and how far it shall run. No one can really help him in this decision, he must practice such shots until judgment comes.

Already the player has been instructed in the task of achieving length and it remains now to discuss with him the methods of controlling run so that he may be able to execute any type of approach shot that appears most likely to succeed.

It is usual to divide approach shots in to three classes:—pitch-and-run, pitch, and cut. The player will be instructed in the details of each shot in turn, but it ought to be pointed out here that this classification is rather misleading, for it is apt to create the impression that there is no other correct way of playing an approach. Leaving out the cut shot for the moment, for it is seldom employed, it may be said that approach shots vary from the pitch-and-run to the pitch. These two shots are the limits of a whole series of shots, and it is really in his ability to play these intermediate shots that the first-class golfer differs most markedly from his fellows.

109

B.—NATURE OF THE SHOT

The pitch-and-run, as its name implies, is played in such a way that there is considerable run after pitching. The trajectory of the ball is low and the running power can be increased by imparting top-spin.

This shot, when properly played, is one of the prettiest in the game, yet in some quarters there is a strange and unwarranted objection to it on the ground that it is fluky. It is argued that contact with the ground during the run is bound to vary in its effect, and that by comparison with the pitch the stroke is in the nature of a gamble. This criticism can best be answered after a consideration of the conditions under which this shot should be played, but it may be said here that the shot should not be confused with a mis-hit, top, or such like; for the latter have, as a rule, a certain amount of bias and the conditions of the course may be all against a running ball.

There are three sets of conditions for which the pitch-and-run is usually the safest shot to play, namely, when the ground is hard, undulating, and wind-swept. The modern ball is so resilient that during hard-baked conditions it is difficult to decide correctly upon the place to pitch a ball for the bounce is so uncertain owing to the back-spin. The effect of back-spin in such circumstances is much more uncertain than that of top-spin, or of absence of spin. If players will practice the pitch-and-run when the fairways are hard they will be amazed to find how truly and strongly the ball will run when the shot is played properly, and how little it is influenced by broken ground, irregularities of the turf and the other small accidents of fate that it may reasonably be expected to encounter.

Again, if a strong wind is blowing there is no shot that is so indifferent to it, especially if the wind be head on or following. Players who have had the good fortune to learn the game on a seaside links usually play this shot extremely well for dire necessity has compelled them to play it so often.

Finally the pitch-and-run is the safest shot to play when the green has to be approached across a series of undulations, except, of course, when the conditions will allow of a pitch on to the green. Played with top-spin the ball will surmount these one by one, whereas a pitched ball may land unfavorably among them and stay there. Especially is this likely to happen when playing on strange courses, for what appears to be a gradual slope up to a green may, on closer inspection, prove to be a series of undulations, and if the conditions are too hard to warrant pitching on the green a stroke can readily be lost by pitching short.

In playing the pitch-and-run the club to use is the mashie, but a jigger or No. 3 iron may be used for the longer shot, or against a strong headwind. Whichever club is used, the method of play is exactly the same.

Finally, the shot is the easiest of all to play as there is really no variation in the method of playing the longer strokes from that of playing the iron. It is in consequence safer and has the further merit of tending to fix a style. Only a genius can employ widely different methods for his clubs and still play well.

C.—SHORT CHIPS

(i) *Introductory*

A chip is a short pitch-and-run with the run almost entirely on the green. There is no cut in the shot and the ball should run straight. There is no wrist movement. The stroke is really a putt, made with a club sufficiently lofted to enable the ball to pitch over the intervening broken ground. A mashie is usually employed, although if the green be large and undulating, and the flag on the side remote from the player, an iron will probably be the safer and more satisfactory club to use.

The object of the shot is to hit the ball straight to the pin and stop it there, not by back-spin but by correctly gauging the strength. Accuracy of length, when the stroke is correctly made, depends partially on delicacy of finger grip. Direction, which is almost equally im-

112

portant, is regulated by the free passage of the left arm in the stroke; thus the stance and grip are very important.

The shot must be completely framed in the player's mind; he must know where the ball is to pitch and how it must behave. There is really no shot more entrancing to practice and none that brings a greater reward.

Usefulness of the shot.—On some courses, the greens are so fiercely bunkered that the long second may bring dire disaster, especially if the wind be troublesome. In such cases many players deem it advisable to play slightly short or to the side for safety, and rely on their skill with the chip shot to lay the ball as near the pin as they could have hoped to do if they had reached the green and played an approach putt from a remote corner.

Again, the short player who has just failed to reach the green may still get on level terms if he has mastered this short approach. And the moral effect on the opponent is important in match play for sooner or later one of these approaches is going down.

This little shot, then, should be taken firmly in hand. Practice can usefully fill up odd moments, and it is seldom difficult to get in a few shots between the matches coming along.

(ii) Preliminaries

Stance.—Slightly open, the left shoulder

pointing straight to the pin. In this shot there will be no pivoting and as it is necessary to get the left hip out of the way when the club meets the ball, the best plan is to do this at the outset by adopting a very open stance.

Feet.—Heels near together. This tends to prevent pivoting and to make the stroke entirely an arm movement.

Weight.—On the left foot. The backward movement of the hands and club must be counterbalanced by having the weight forward on the left.

Ball.—Opposite the left heel and immediately beneath the eye.

Grip.—The back of the left hand should face the hole and the right hand should be on the side of the shaft. Only the thumb and first finger of each hand should be gripping at all firmly (*see* grip for putt).

Elbows.—The left shoulder should be raised and the left elbow bent, and projecting towards the hole; the right elbow should be tucked in against the hip bone.

(iii) Playing Instructions
(for ordinary chip)

1.—By means of the left, push the club-head back along the line of flight, keeping the face shut, and the club-head brushing the grass.

2.—At the same time make a slight lateral movement of the right hip.

3.—Complete the stroke by a reverse move-ment of the left arm and right hip, the right hand giving firmness to the stroke at impact only (Figs. 98, 99).

(iv) Notes on the Instructions

1. At the finish of the back-swing the back of the left hand will face the ground and the toe of the club will point only slightly upwards.

2. Both shoulders should be firmly braced in the address and kept rigid throughout the stroke. There will be no pivoting, but the lateral move-ment of the right hip, which is really the prime movement, will induce a slight see-saw move-ment of the shoulders. Thus in the back-swing the left shoulder will dip very slightly and rise slightly in the forward swing. The essence of this shot is rigidity of the left shoulder through-out. The shoulders maintain the same line rela-tive to the ball.

3. Keep the right hand out of this shot. It is essential that back-spin be avoided. If the right interferes in the back-swing the club-head will be lifted, instead of brushing the grass, and a vertical or descending blow will be delivered. This may produce a foozle through hitting the ground behind, but in any case it will produce back-spin.

The trajectory of the ball must be low, for the

ball has to travel a relatively long way after pitching.

4. Played well, the shot is smooth and slow. At impact the left hand is taking the club firmly through the ball, and if the mind be concentrated on this "through" movement of the left, there is a greater chance of the right being cut out until impact. The face of the club should finish open.

5. When played properly, with rhythm, the player will feel

> (*a*) that the ball has been thrown rather than hit;
>
> (*b*) that the work has been done by the shoulders.

(*v*) *Playing Instructions for increased Run*

1. Proceed as above but at impact follow through by turning the left wrist over towards the hole.

The effect is to keep the face of the club shut after impact. The toe of the club at the finish of the stroke will point towards the hole. The right hand will climb over the left, and the effect will be to push the ball and impart top-spin.

Increased run can also be obtained by using a straight-faced club; a putting cleek is very useful for this purpose. It is advisable to use a club with little loft if the stroke be up a slope.

116

D.—Longer Running Approaches

(Figs. 102-107)

General Principles.—Having mastered the small running approach, and so become fully conversant with the principles involved in keeping a ball down and in imparting top-spin, the player can proceed to longer shots. The ball has now to be hit harder, but the player is warned against the natural tendency to do this by striking faster: he should swing slowly.

He must proceed exactly as he did with the short approach. As soon as he finds he cannot get the length he must alter his grip and stance, etc., as suggested in the accompanying table. Whenever a running approach goes wrong the player should look to his grip and stance as the explanation can often be found there. If the practice proceeds as suggested from short shots to long through intermediate stages, there is less likelihood of the shots being ruined by snatching and pressing. A leisurely swing is required for running shots with, however, great firmness of wrist at impact and after.

Another advantage results from practicing the short shots first in that it is always easier to make the necessary adjustments if the practice has proceeded in that order.

It is possible to indicate in only a general way the nature of the variations that are desirable in playing the longer shots. It would be useless to

117

suggest the length of shot for which each variation is best adapted, as lengths are relative to the player.

TABLE OF VARIATIONS FROM THE SHORT CHIP

Grip	*Left*—gradually creeping over the shaft. *Right*—keeping to the right of the shaft and gradually gripping more firmly.
Stance	*Fairly open*—gradually becoming almost square. *Feet together*—gradually widening.
Weight	*Mainly on left*—gradually shifting on to the right.
Elbow	*Left*—bent forward, gradually straightening until it hugs the left side. *Right*—hugging right side—no change.
Face of Club..	Shut throughout.
Back-Swing ...	Flat throughout and slow.

118

CHAPTER XVI

SHORT APPROACHES—THE PITCH SHOT

(Figs. 108-120)

A.—INTRODUCTORY

The Shot.—This shot arises within about 120 yards of the pin and the club employed is usually the mashie-niblick. If there be doubt about ability to get the length a more powerful club should be used, such as the mashie or jigger.

The occasions when this shot has to be played occur frequently. During the winter, and at other times when the turf is soft, it is usually best to pitch right up to or within a few yards of the green; while it is imperative to use the shot if the green be guarded by cross bunkers.

The great concern of the shot is to curtail the run by imparting back-spin. Once the player has taken the correct grip and adopted the right swing he can leave the rest to the club-head. The less he thinks about his own part in the stroke and the more he leaves to the club the better he will play. But the grip is important, and it is necessary to get a correct conception of the path to be traversed by the club-head, for it is by attention to these details that control over the run is secured. But, once these matters are mastered, the main concern really becomes the correct gauging of length.

B.—PRELIMINARIES

General Note.—In this shot the player is concerned mainly with the manipulation of the club-head at impact and while contact is being maintained. Hence the preliminaries to the stroke are of enormous importance; for the exact movement of the blade at this point depends on the twist or movement of the wrists and this, in turn, on the grip and stance.

It has been thought most helpful, then, to indicate to the player the directions in which the grip and stance, etc., differ from those employed for the ordinary pitch-and-run, and to leave it to him to work out his own salvation. At this stage he will already have been experimenting to secure a controlled run and needs only, perhaps, to have his own discoveries confirmed.

It may be said, however, beforehand that the blade has to be kept open both at impact and during the period of contact and all the instructions here given are designed to enable this to be done. If the player keeps this fact in mind the reason for each variation will be more or less apparent.

120

TABLE.

	Comparison with pitch-and-run.	
Stance	(1) Slightly more open (2) More behind the ball	For chips, but for longer shots the stances approximate to those for the pitch-and-run.
Weight	More on right throughout.	
Grip	(1) Left hand: in front of shaft—one knuckle showing. (2) Right hand: on top.	
Elbows	Both well tucked in.	
Club-face ...	Natural lie of club: on no account open.	
Swing	Faster and more upright.	

C.—THE CHIP

(Figs. 108-112)

This small shot occurs when an obstacle has to be surmounted and the run cut short, as often happens for example round a well-bunkered green. The object is to produce back-spin. For other short chips the pitch-and-run is strongly advocated, as being the less likely to lose the player a stroke through error in length. A back-spinning ball is always liable to behave

121

unexpectedly on pitching, whereas the ball with top-spin can be relied upon.

Follow the method of play for the pitch-and-run chip but adopt the variations in stance and grip, etc., suggested in the above table. The increased loft on the club will get the ball up. Be sure to keep the club-face shut in the back-swing and, if the grip be correct, the club-face will finish open, as it must do to impart the back-spin.

The player must note that in the back-swing, even for these short shots, his right hip must lock and the left shoulder must be held. The upper part of his body must be rock-like, and the movement must be from the hips downwards. If he can get this hip movement going in the chips it will creep into the longer strokes as well.

When coming on to the ball the action of the blade should be that of a footballer kicking a ball. After impact his foot is moving parallel to the ground, and so back-spin is imparted. If the toe of the boot were to rise again under the ball the effect would be a sort of sling difficult to time and gauge. In the case of chips the ball must be hit in the down-swing.

D.—PLAYING INSTRUCTIONS FOR ORDINARY SHOTS

(Figs. 113-118)

1. By means of the left hand bring the club back along the line of flight, making at the same

time a slight lateral and upward movement of the right hip.

2. Hold the right knee and lift the hands upward, without allowing the right hip to sway away from the line of flight.

3. Bring the club-head down with the left and drive it downward under the ball, letting the club-head take its natural course along the line to the hole.

NOTES

1. The left heel rises slightly during the making of the strokes.

2. In the pivot, the twisting is made at the knees rather than at the hips, and the left knee bends forward towards the ball and not inward towards the right knee, there being a fair amount of weight on the ball of the left toe.

3. Do not let the hands sweep round the body when they lift, as they cannot be got back again (Figs. 81, 82). If the club-head be taken back along the line of flight a descending blow can be given which is necessary to get back-spin.

4. The wrists should not deliberately bend at the top of the swing.

5. The club-head in the down-swing gets on to the line of flight sooner than it does in making the pitch-and-run, and continues in it. At impact the wrist movement is not in the nature of a scoop. The wrist work must be firm.

6. At the finish the hands are well forward,

123

low down and rather in front of the body, the
result of trying to keep the blade open. Both
elbows should be pointing to the ground. The
shaft should be almost vertical.

7. The weight at the finish is mainly on the
right as it is essential to keep the body back at
impact and after.

8. Aim to drop the ball in line with the pin.

Practice Hints.—Most players look forward
with pleasure to the season when the conditions
favor the playing of a mashie-niblick pitch, for
no stroke is more satisfying than a firm, con-
fident, lofted shot that drops near the pin and
stays there. In winter, then, or during a spell
of wet weather, the mashie-niblick pitch for the
shorter distances, or a mashie pitch for the
longer, is the shot to play, for the ball can be
relied upon not to bounce far after pitching.

All approach shots should be made easily;
there should be no straining after length. If the
player be in doubt he should use a club of
greater power—the mashie for the mashie-niblick, a No. 3 iron for the mashie and so on—and
should play a restrained shot with it. On no account should he endeavor to get extra length by
shutting the club-face, for the ball will run in
that case, whereas it is necessary that it should
not do so. If, however, a head wind is blowing
slightly from the left he would shut the face to a
degree so as to hold the ball up and prevent it
from drifting, for that is a legitimate use of the

club; in such a case the wind would put the necessary brake on the ball and curtail the run.

It is a good plan when practicing pitches with either the mashie or mashie-niblick to select for the purpose a green guarded by a formidable bunker and to endeavor to put the ball into it. In most cases, if the player be honest in his intentions, he will be surprised to find that the ball gets up and sails over the bunker on to the green. This is because in his endeavor to effect his purpose he drove the club-head *down*, and that is exactly how the mashie and mashie-niblick have to be played to get the ball up.

In wet weather a good player welcomes a bunker or other trouble intervening between him and the hole as it forces him to make the very shot he would play if the bunker were not there. It is a good thing, then, if the player can conjure up a bunker in his mind when a pitch is to be made, as it may help him to make the right shot.

Common Pitching Faults.—Errors in pitching with the mashie and mashie-niblick arise normally out of three faults:—

1. Lack of faith in one's self. In the down-swing the arms and wrists become flabby through the determination giving way: there is a fear that the shot will be too strong. A short, uncontrolled shot results—really a mis-hit.

2. Lack of faith in the club-head. The

125

player gets the idea in his head that some special lofting movement on his part is required to get the ball up—some sort of scoop of the club-head to be brought about by a twist, or what not, of the wrists. The result of this brain-wave is normally either a scuttled shot through hitting the ball on the up-swing or a short skied ball.

3. Lack of hip movement. The player has been relying too much on his wrists. In the down-swing there is usually a reversal of the proper body movement, for as the arms and wrists are coming down and through with the shot the hips are actually swaying away from the hole. The finish is as shown in Figs. 38, 39.

CHAPTER XVII

SHORT APPROACHES—THE CUT SHOT

(Figs. 121-124)

A.—PLAYING INSTRUCTIONS

THE preparations for this shot are the same as for the Pitch shot except that the club-face is laid farther back and the stance is slightly more open and more behind the ball. The club used is generally the mashie-niblick, but the niblick or mashie may be employed: it is often a question of the player's mood at the moment.

In the back-swing the hands are taken away from the body, and in the down-swing brought back so that the club-head hits the ball a descending and glancing blow from right to left. In all other respects the shot resembles the pitch.

It should be noted that the ball will not take the line of the club-head but will fly more towards the hole; also, that on pitching it will break to the right, and allowance must be made for this.

B.—USES OF THE SHOT

The occasions when this shot can be used advantageously are very rare. There are two situations, however, when it is perhaps the best shot to employ, namely:—

> (a) when the ball is lying at the foot of a mound and
>
> (b) when the ball is embedded in thick grass near the green.

The advantage of the shot in both cases lies partly in the fact that the ball is made to get up quickly, but in the latter case there are other advantages, and, as the shot occurs fairly frequently on some courses, it may be well to discuss it more fully.

Short Chips out of long grass (Figs. 121-124). This is one of the trickiest shots to play and calls for constant practice. The blade should be laid well back, and the grip with the left hand should be almost under the shaft; the stance very open and well behind the ball. The swing should be upright, and if the heel of the club leads, the oblique right to left blow will get the ball up sharply. This is the best way of circumventing the resisting power of the grass; a shut face is fatal in such a situation.

A variant is to play what is virtually the explosion shot (*see* Niblick, p. 137). In this case the club descends obliquely as before and strikes the ground an inch or so behind the ball. This raises the turf sharply and the ball is "dunted" up and out. This is a most effective stroke if only a short distance has to be covered. A point to note with regard to this shot is the tendency

128

to strike too gently. Bring the club down firmly with the left and bang the heel into the ground and out again.

C.—OTHER CONSIDERATIONS

The cut shot should be employed only for chips, or when trees have to be lofted over or sliced round.

For longer shots the stroke is not to be recommended if the object is to curtail run, and it may be said that in modern first-class golf the stroke is seldom played except for chips. If it be desired to hold up a long shot against a right to left slope a little cut should be imparted for the purpose, but in that case there is no alternative stroke.

The cut shot is not for beginners although, like a distemper, it afflicts all ambitious young golfers. Every golfer must learn it sooner or later, and, sooner or later, he learns when not to use it. It is safe to say that for many years he will employ it too often. As we grow older we realize that "fancy" shots do not pay.

Error in making the cut shot can arise from two causes, viz., either from misjudging the length or from mis-hitting the ball and so producing a scuttle. The latter error is due to lack of skill or lack of practice. Misjudgment of length is due either to lack of unity of purpose, i.e., concentration, or to lack of courage; in other words, the player either forgets to hit, or is

129

afraid to hit. In either case, the ball lands in the hazard that it is intended to clear. It is difficult to think of two things at once and that is why the pitch shot is to be preferred; for the player, provided he knows how to play the shot, is not concerned with the two-fold task of putting on back-spin and judging length, but only with the latter. A simple shot is always easier than a complex one and is therefore to be preferred, especially if, as in this case, it is equally efficacious.

In the days of the gutty ball, pitching, with or without cut, was a high art. Played by a master, the inert ball seldom ran more than a few yards. Thus pitching was sedulously practiced, for it was a most profitable stroke. The introduction of the rubber core, however, and its subsequent evolution in the direction of increased resiliency have changed the method of playing short approaches. On soft courses and during the wetter seasons, the pitcher can still get in deadly work, but when the ground is even moderately hard, his skill is apt to find little outlet. The present lively ball simply will not behave on hard courses as the older ball did. Even if dropped dead by a high lofting shot, it will seldom fail to bounce across and so over-run even the largest green. If played short to allow for the run it is obvious that there must be no cut on the ball if it is to run straight. The cut approach, then, is as good as dead, and even the pitch must be used with caution when the fairway is hard.

This change in the ball has brought about a change in golfing architecture as well, for the old cross-bunker guarding the green is seldom met with nowadays. It has also brought into being the mashie-niblick. Confronted, then, with an approach shot to-day the player has to decide first of all whether the shot can be a pitch-and-run or whether it must be pitched. If the latter he will take a mashie-niblick and rely on the extra loft to do for him what had to be done in the gutty days by the cut shot with the mashie.

D.—CONCLUSION

As a final word on approach play, spoken in a general way, the player is strongly urged to play some form of pitch-and-run whenever the ground is hard and there are no obstacles to surmount. To play pitch shots under such conditions, as is the habit of some players, betokens a lack of real knowledge of the pitch-and-run—or perhaps, a lack of imagination. Many such players hold the view that the effective run-ups of their opponents are really mis-hits, or if not, are played because they cannot play a skillful pitch.

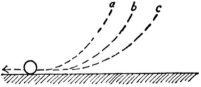

FIG. 125.—COMPARISON OF ARCS DESCRIBED BY CLUB-HEAD IN (a) CUT-SHOT, (b) PITCH, (c) PITCH-AND-RUN.

If the pitch-and-run be impossible then the pitch is to be preferred to the cut shot. In any case when once the player has made up his mind he should have faith in his judgment and strike with courage. For if he falters at the last he may indeed get the length but he is sure to lose some measure of control of the run through the wrists not going firmly through. Flabbiness in the wrist action is the inevitable result of indecision and is invariably followed by an uncontrolled run; an uncontrolled run usually spells trouble.

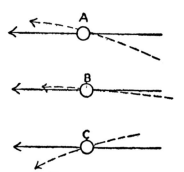

FIG. 126.—PLANS OF ARCS DESCRIBED BY CLUB-HEAD IN (A) PITCH-AND-RUN, (B) PITCH, (C) CUT SHOT.

Comparison of the swings.—It may help to impress on the mind the essential differences in the path of the club-head in the down-swing if diagrams 125 and 126 are studied.

FINAL HINTS FOR SHORT SHOTS

1. *Ground the club on the heel.*
2. *Keep the hands low.*

3. *The knees should be bent in the address and never fully straightened.*
4. *In the back-swing the club face should be shut.*
5. *At impact the club-face should be slightly shut, except for the cut shot.*
6. *After impact the club-face will open through a slight backward turn of the left wrist.*
7. *Take the club-head back along the line of flight. The face should be kept shut.*
8. *The back-swing must be resisted by the right hip.*
9. *Don't roll the left wrist until the club-head is lifted—that is, until the line-of-flight movement has finished.*
10. *Hit down and through the ball.*

CHAPTER XVIII

THE NIBLICK

(Figs. 127-130)

The Club and its Uses.—The chief use of the niblick is to make a lofted shot out of a bunker or long grass. In either case considerable resistance has to be overcome and the ball has to be made to get up quickly: hence the blade must be heavy and have considerable loft. A light niblick is to all intents and purposes a mashie-niblick and is therefore a duplication of that club. The shaft should be stiff and of mashie length.

The width of the blade is rather important. For some shots the blade has to be driven deep into the sand and obviously a very broad pattern would be a drawback. On the other hand, it is sometimes necessary to cut across the ball, and this cannot be done successfully or confidently with a narrow blade. For these two reasons, then, the ideal niblick is very little broader in the face than a mashie.

It may be opportune to mention here that great distance with such a heavy club as the niblick cannot be expected and the player may find it possible to get the ball up with a speedier club and so recover lost ground. This possibility should always be considered when a bunker shot presents itself.

But apart from the uses of a niblick in cutting through sand and stones when the ball is lying badly in a bunker, and in cutting through grass, heather and the like, there is another use to which the niblick can often be put with great advantage and that is in making short approaches in situations where it is fatal to over-run. The special advantage possessed by the club for this purpose arises out of its weight. Every experienced golfer knows that the behavior of a ball when struck quickly by a light club differs widely from its behavior when struck by a heavy one. In the former case the ball has been hit, while in the latter it has been slung. The quickly hit ball is alive, for good or evil; it is unsteady on its feet and its contact with the ground emphasizes every weakness in the execution of the stroke. All this appears to result from the increased pace with which the ball leaves the club-head.

On the other hand in the slow-moving niblick shot the compression effect is so slight that the ball has no more life in it than if launched from a sling. The difficulty in the shot lies in gauging the length: there is a tendency to be short.

PRELIMINARIES

General Note.—Usually the player is unable to take just such a stance as he would like when playing out of a bunker; and in other ways, too, the special circumstances of the case may compel him to depart from his usual method of attack. Consequently the advice given below cannot always be followed and must accordingly be looked upon as a counsel of perfection in preparing to play every type of niblick shot.

Stance.—Open and well behind. The ball should be opposite the left toe and vertically beneath the eye.

Feet.—Not very near together. The left should almost point in the direction the ball must fly and the right should be at right angles to the line of flight.

Weight.—Mainly on the right. Consequently this foot especially should be dug in until a firm foothold is secured. This is important, for the niblick is a heavy club and great strain is thrown on the right foot throughout the swing. If this foot slips the club is apt to be driven into the sand in rear of the intended spot.

Grip.—The left hand should be on the side of the shaft facing the hole, with one knuckle showing. The right hand should be well on top. Both should grip firmly.

Both hands have crept forward over the shaft towards the hole but at the finish of the stroke the left will be on top and the right beneath. It must not be assumed that the grip has slackened and allowed the shaft to rotate in the hands; the explanation is given later.

136

PLAYING INSTRUCTIONS FOR BUNKER SHOTS

General Notes.—When a ball is lying in a bunker it may be possible to treat it as an ordinary mashie-niblick shot and that club may in fact be used. Sometimes, however, it may be lying very badly; in a foot-print, perhaps, or behind a stone. In such a case it may be impossible to bring the club-head into contact with the ball at all, or, if so, only so as to drive it further into the sand. The proper method of play here is to bury the club-head in the sand an inch or even two inches behind the ball and so "dunt" it up into the air without the blade actually coming into contact with it. This shot is usually termed the Explosion shot, for the sand usually flies upwards as if a small mine had been fired beneath it. It is surprising how far a ball can be propelled in this way, and how sharply it can be made to rise. Not only is this the only effective way of playing a heavily embedded ball in a sand bunker but the player will find it most effectual in dislodging a ball from a hole or rabbit scrape in a bunker face, or from long grass (*see* p. 128).

There are thus two types of shot possible in a sand bunker and the instructions vary slightly for each.

(*a*) FOR CUT SHOT WITH NIBLICK

1. By means of the left hand bring the club-head widely back slightly outside the line of

flight and lift to a little beyond the vertical position.

2. Return it by the same hand so as to cut across the ball from right to left with firm wrists.

NOTES

1. As the idea of the stroke is to cut across the ball and to keep the blade open there must be no knuckling over of the right. Instead the right should actually rotate the other way from impact onwards.

2. Hence the grip is very important, for such a movement cannot be made if in the address the left hand is above the shaft and the right at the right-hand side. Before entering the bunker the player should ground his club, lay back the face, and then take up his grip as suggested above.

3. The hands must go forward and the club-head should be driven forwards and upwards and not left in the sand.

4. Most weight, at the finish, should be on the right foot—but at the top of the swing it is on the left.

(b) EXPLOSION SHOT

1. The shot is played exactly like the cut shot, except that the blade is driven into the sand some inch or so behind the ball.

138

NOTES

1. The club-head remains buried.

2. The distance from the ball of the spot aimed at will be greater if the sand is loose and light, and less if it is hard and heavy.

3. It is important to remember that this shot must be a powerful one and therefore the back-swing must be wide and upright and the pivot extensive, for, unless this is so, the blow may not be effective.

(c) IN LONG GRASS

1. Exactly as for the cut shot (already dealt with).

NOTES

1. The blade in this case strikes the ball a glancing blow from right to left and so cuts it up.

2. The resistance to the blade is much less than when the club-face is shut.

3. It may be advisable at times to play the Explosion shot and get the ball up without actually striking it.

139

CHAPTER XIX

PUTTING

A.—THE CLUB

Type.—For all players and for all occasions
the straight-faced aluminium club is preferable
to a putting cleek. There are three main reasons
why this is so. In the first place the stance is
taken up uniformly, for the grounding of the
broad, flat sole indicates automatically the correct position. This is of great importance, for a
slight variation in the stance, whether ahead or
in rear of the normal, may seriously affect the
success of a long approach putt: if the player
is slightly ahead of the correct position he may
drive the ball down and so be short, and if he is
in rear he may put on top spin and so over-run;
in both cases he is liable to mis-hit.

Secondly, the absence of loft on the aluminium
putter eliminates error that may arise from the
production of back-spin. Most putting cleeks,
on the other hand, have a certain degree of loft
and the ball can thereby be made to leave the
ground, can be given back-spin, and so on; thus
judgment of strength is made more complicated
and uncertain than it need be.

Thirdly, there is another count to be laid to the charge of the putting cleek more serious than the others and this appears to put it almost entirely out of court. It arises out of its similarity to an iron. This similarity tends to create in the mind an impulse to make an upright swing and so to give the ball a descending blow. This not only emphasizes the back-spin, but it may make the ball jump into the air, or it may drive it into the ground, thus bringing about serious errors in both length and direction. The aluminium club, on the other hand, through the size and flatness of its sole, compels, or at any rate tends to produce a flat back-swing which, as we shall see later, is one of the most essential points in the putting stroke.

Weight.—A suitable weight for a putter is 10 ozs. It is a mistake to use a light club. The stroke tends in that case to become a hit and rhythm is destroyed. The essence of a correct putt is the firm push through the ball, and this is difficult to do with a light putter.

Shaft.—A sensitive shaft tends to judgment of length, and care should be taken not to alter the length or thickness of the grip, for the sensitiveness may be affected thereby. The lie of the club should be fairly upright so that the player can stand comfortably near the ball.

B.—PRELIMINARIES

(*See* Figs. 131-134)

Stance.—Very open, with the heels together. The ball should be opposite the left heel and so near as to be beneath the eye. The head should be down but the body should not be unduly inclined forward. The left foot carries more weight than the right. Both hands are tucked close in to the body.

Grip.—The left hand is on the left of the shaft so that the back of the hand faces the hole. The left shoulder should be up, and the left elbow should be bent and pointing to the hole. The grip is mainly with the thumb and forefinger.

The right hand should be down the side of the shaft and the grip should be very light, just sufficient to steady the club. The right elbow should be tucked in and touching the right hip. The elbow never moves from this position during the stroke. The two shoulders should be in a line with the hole.

All these instructions are very important in view of the fact that the stroke is a left-handed stroke and requires a free and uninterrupted swing of the left arm.

C.—THE STROKE

1. Using chiefly the left hand, ground the

142

club in front of the ball at right angles to the proposed initial direction the ball has to take.

2. At once lift it over the ball and ground it behind.

3. Without pausing make a slight backward movement of the right hip and at the same time by means of the left hand push the club-head back, with a flat arc, along the line of flight, keeping the face of the club shut.

4. Complete the stroke by a slightly forward movement of the right hip and a forward movement of the left hand and wrist, keeping the wrist firm.

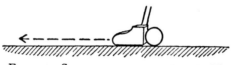

FIG. 135.—SHOWING FLAT ARC DESCRIBED BY PUTTER IN BACK-SWING.

D.—NOTES ON THE STROKE

1. The grounding of the club before and behind the ball is really accompanied by a slightly forward movement of the right hip. These movements take the place of the waggle: a really rhythmic stroke cannot be made from a stationary position. Hence the putt stroke really begins the moment the player lifts the putter to ground it in front of the ball; from that point onwards there should be no hesitation or interruption in the stroke.

143

2. If the left shoulder be kept up, the passage of the left hand in both sections of the stroke is uniform, and a flat arc is described without jabbing the ground at impact. One feels on many occasions, in taking up the stance to putt, that the feet are glued, as it were, to the ground, and that the stroke must be made entirely with the arms. We know instinctively that such strokes will be little better than snatches. This cramped feeling is due entirely to the fact that the shoulders are not braced. Directly the player corrects this he will feel that his legs are automatically relaxed. The movement of the right hip, so essential to good putting, can now be made and the spell of snatching should give way to smooth, rhythmic swinging.

3. The left hand is bent slightly backwards towards the hole in the address, and in short putts this disposition of forearm, wrist and hand may be said to remain unchanged. As length increases the left wrist comes more into the stroke until at the limit of the back-swing the hand is in line with the forearm. This should be looked upon as the limit of the wrist movement.

4. The right elbow does not move relatively to the body. As the right hip moves backwards and forwards the elbow moves with it. The right wrist, of course, bends but takes no conscious part in the stroke until impact, when it firms up and supports the left.

144

5. The backward movement of the club-head is stopped by the left shoulder and not by the wrists. This is specially important. In order to bring this about the right hip should be braced so as to hold the shoulders, which should not deviate from their original line: that is, there is no pivoting. There is, however, a distinct see-saw movement, and when the player is putting well he will be conscious that he is putting with his shoulders, which means to say that his left arm and left shoulder are one and do not move relatively to one another.

6. The weight must be well forward on the left foot to preserve the balance throughout the stroke.

7. The player's head must not move until the ball has left the club.

E.—ON THE PUTTING GREEN

Rhythm.—Throughout this book the player is advised not to make a stroke without having definitely framed the shot in his mind; that is, he must have determined where the ball is to pitch and how it is subsequently to behave.

On the putting green this advice holds with equal force, for unless the player has made a mental note of the strength and direction, that is, unless he can see clearly in his mind's eye the whole journey of the ball from start to finish, he cannot shape the shot as a whole and so will

145

not make a rhythmic swing. If there is no rhythm the stroke is a mis-hit whatever the result may be. Rhythm is the essence of good putting.

Some players have unusual skill on the putting green and are sometimes referred to as born putters. Of some of these we learn that they seldom practice putting, and their skill is in consequence generally looked upon as a natural gift. In a sense this may be true, but the fact of the matter is really this, that they have the valuable and unusual capacity of being able to visualize the putting green from the ball to the hole when they are actually making the stroke. Thus a clear-cut message, as it were, is transmitted to the muscles concerned and a correct rhythmic swing is the result. Good billiard players seem also to have a fine attunement between nerves and muscles and this, among golfers, is usually the accompaniment of fine physical fitness. When we are tired we become jaded and nerve-weary and our rhythm is apt to leave us.

We need not despair if we do not appear to possess this natural gift, for it can be acquired; to say that good putters are born, not made, is all nonsense. It is generally admitted that the first-class American players are, to a man, good putters; in fact some of them are almost uncanny. On inquiry, we find that they were not always so, and that their skill on the green is really the

146

result of hard practice and deep concentration; indeed, it may be said that their powers of concentration are the outcome of the practice.

The player, then, must first get a good putting style, that is to say, his putting stroke must be mechanically sound. The advantages of the left arm stroke advocated in this chapter are twofold: first, it is the logical conclusion to the series of left arm strokes advocated for the other clubs, and, secondly, as the stroke is regulated by the left shoulder—itself controlled by the right hip—length can be gauged.

Having the method correct, he can now proceed to acquire rhythm by putting at an object rather than into something; in other words he will concentrate first of all on direction only. The slow easy rhythmic stroke will soon come, and the sight of the ball running firmly and smoothly will compensate the player for any drudgery entailed.

The Approach Putt.—Opinions differ as to what constitutes an approach putt. It cannot be defined as a putt of over a certain length, for the nature of the green comes into the question. Speaking roughly, one might say that on a level putting green the minimum length might be put at about 3 yards: within that distance the player has a reasonable chance of holing.

Experience will teach the player the main

147

points to be taken into account in determining
the strength and direction—such points as the
direction in which the grass has been cut, the
rise and fall of the ground, the degree of mois-
ture, and so on—but one or two special considerations might be mentioned here, as due attention is not always given to them. Every player
should examine carefully the nature of the green
immediately round the hole—say, within a
radius of a yard; many an approach putt fails
to drop into the tin through neglect of this preliminary survey. Especially is this likely to happen when the ball is having a struggle to reach
the hole, for then it is readily influenced by small
indentations, slopes, stubbles, and the like.

Besides, it is always well to know whether the
yard putt that may remain to be negotiated is
likely to be difficult or otherwise, if the approach be strong, weak, wide, etc.

Another point to note is the greater effect of
an undulation on a slow ball as compared with a
fast in turning it from its course. Therefore
take more note of the undulations near the hole
than of those near the ball.

As a final word on the approach putt remember that judgment of length is of far more importance than judgment of direction. Whenever three putts are taken on a green it is almost
invariably the result of an error in strength in
the approach putt. "Never up, never in," was a
useful slogan in the gutty days when errors in

148

strength were seldom great and when direction was more easily maintained by the more inert ball. The chances were that if you could get the ball up to the hole it would go in.

But the modern lively ball may go five feet past through an error of judgment that would have sent the gutty only as many inches astray. And this return putt, as we all know, is one of the most tantalizing tasks the modern golfer sets himself. It is only common sense that a ball that reaches the hole has a chance of dropping in which the short ball never has, but if the slogan "Never up, never in" flashes through the player's mind as he is making his stroke, it will almost always adversely affect his judgment and make him over-run.

Coupled with this question of length is the question of deciding whether to play to hole or to play to lie dead. Whatever the decision, there should be no wavering. It is really best to play to hole; not because a ball in the tin is worth two on the lip, but because the hole is a definite objective and this tends to clearness of thought and purpose.

The Short Putt.—A putt of five feet or so is the most nerve-wracking stroke in golf: you feel it ought to be possible to send the ball into the hole whereas experience tells you it is just as likely to stay out. If you can hole it, a stroke will be saved or perhaps a hole won—it may even be that the match hangs on the stroke. Thus the mind is disturbed. All sorts of ideas occur to one for holing—a push, jab, hit, slice, pull, slack wrists, taut wrists, stiff forearm, long grip, short grip, tight grip, upright stance, crouch, and so on—the brain putting in great work. The result is that the player can come to no definite decision and a mis-hit follows.

Practically every missed putt is due to a mis-hit, and the mis-hit is due to lack of rhythm, and the lack of rhythm is the result of inability to visualize the shot and to concentrate until it is made.

First of all take the line carefully to the back of the hole; if there must be borrow allow for it on the understanding that the stroke is going to be firm. Select a spot a few inches in front of the ball in the line the ball must take. Visualize the path. Strike firmly so as to drive the ball over this spot and don't look up. If this happens the stroke-motif will be interrupted and a mis-hit will result. Be firm and be up.

CHAPTER XX

THE STYMIE

IT is not the easiest of tasks to advise on the playing of stymies, as the shot varies so much with distance from the hole and from the obstructing ball. Also the nature of the green further complicates the problem, whether it be fast or slow, uphill or downhill, undulating or smooth, and so on. There is also the further complication arising from the state of the score, for obviously one can play more boldly for a half than for a win. In playing a stymie, as in playing a putt, the player must be guided by his own judgment and experience.

It is rather hard luck, after outplaying the opponent up to the green, to be set the task of negotiating a stymie in order to retain one's advantage. Thus most people approach the task in anything but a composed state of mind, and it is probably due to this rankling feeling that so large a percentage of failures is due.

The advice in this chapter must of necessity be of a very general nature. It would be best, perhaps, to consider a few typical cases and to leave the player to find out the limits for himself.

Case 1.—In Fig. 136 the opponent's ball is near the lip—say 3 or 4 inches away. The ball

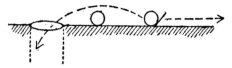

FIG. 136.—STYMIE NEAR THE HOLE.

must be lofted directly into the hole. The mashie-niblick should be used for the purpose.

Case 2.—In Fig. 137 the opponent's ball is a

FIG. 137.—OPPONENT'S BALL A FOOT OR
MORE FROM THE HOLE.

foot or so from the hole. The ball should be lofted so as to run into the hole, the mashie-niblick being again employed.

Case 3.—In Fig. 138, length must be got and

FIG. 138.—LOFTING WITH MASHIE—THE
HOLE BEING SEVERAL YARDS AWAY.

the intervening ball cleared; therefore a mashie is the best club to use.

Case 4.—In Fig. 139, length has to be got, and an iron is the best club to use.

FIG. 139.—LOFTING WITH AN IRON, THE
OBSTRUCTING BALL BEING NEAR THE
PLAYER'S BALL.

How to Play the Shot.—Treat the stroke as either a putt or pitch-and-run. Bring the club back parallel to the ground, keeping the face shut, and return it along the same path, using the left hand throughout. The grip and stance must be exactly as described for those strokes (pp. 113-114).

On no account must the swing be at all upright; there must be no back-spin on the ball, for length is the chief matter to be gauged.

The mashie-niblick was suggested for the shorter shots because it is essential to gauge strength accurately. This is not so easily done with the niblick on account of its extreme loft; further, it feels rather unfamiliar and clumsy when short delicate work is required.

For the longer shots the mashie and iron were recommended because length has to be obtained and it is most easily gauged by a club that keeps the ball in the air for as short a space as possible.

Practice.—Every one should practice run-ups on the green with iron and mashie. After all, the action is exactly that for putting, strength being the only element that differs. It is a useful stroke for other occasions than stymies, and experience stored away in one's head at any rate begets confidence even if it is too dim and remote to produce accuracy. A common experience on big greens is a considerable depression immediately in front of the ball with a subsequent long stretch to the pin. If the player

153

selects a light iron, he can escape the depression and so gauge the length more accurately. Sometimes, too, an old partially subsided flag hole may intervene and must be avoided.

Above all things, the player should notice that the club will do all the lifting without his aid. If he will keep his own head down and the club-head brushing the grass in both sections of the swing, using his left to keep the face shut, he has little to fear. The ball will run as straight as a putt.

As a final word, he should spend a few odd moments from time to time on a green or indoors noticing the effect on the ball of both flat and upright swings with the iron, mashie and mashie-niblick; not with any other object in view than to learn the effect on the ball as regards production of back-spin and its behavior generally. This knowledge will help him more clearly to understand what happens when he is playing through the green. He cannot know too much about the effect of the club for, usually, we all know too little. Really, the more we can sense the reaction of the ball to the club, to slight variations in loft, to variations in point of impact, the greater becomes our capacity to cope with unusual situations as they arise. We drink more deeply, too, of the philosophy of the game, we get more enjoyment from it, and so come to treat it with increased respect.

154

CHAPTER XXI

AWKWARD STANCES

IN his practice spells, the player usually makes the conditions as easy for himself as possible by selecting level stances, easy lies, and so on. In all this he is very wise, for his chief aim at the outset should be to induce an easy rhythmic hip swing and this is most readily achieved when the mind is not worried over niceties.

But once the swings are going smoothly, he should stiffen up the practice conditions. He should begin by giving himself close lies, closer than he would ordinarily expect in a round, and he should persevere until he can get the ball away as cleanly as from the others. This is a most profitable form of practice, for it will give him great confidence when a close lie has to be tackled in a match. The tendency of the beginner in such a case is to press, to dip the body, and so mis-hit. Steadiness and confidence are required, that is all, and these can only be acquired by practice.

If he plays habitually on an inland course, this practice will fit him to cope with most lies that he is likely to encounter on the fairway. And not only so, but he may learn something else of great value; with these close lies, he may learn to play his irons with that degree of push that is so desirable and is so difficult to do when the ball is lying favorably.

But in almost every round there are other types of lies and stances than these, and on most seaside courses they usually occur very frequently. They may be classified as follows: (a) Standing below the ball, (b) standing above the ball, (c) downhill lie, (d) uphill lie. In addition, there may be combinations of these.

Ordinarily this kind of stance and lie are overlooked in the practice spells, and it is not quite obvious why it should be so. Certainly there are few seaside courses that do not present a wide variety of such lies on the fairway, and it is very important that the player who has to play on these courses should know how best to cope with them. Of course, experience would teach him, for he would be compelled to think out for himself conditions of stance and swing. But there are many players who play on such courses only occasionally, and the object of a book of this kind is to give them as many short cuts as possible.

To begin with, a player cannot get the length that he can when the conditions are normal, no matter how assiduously he may practice. But unless he practices, he cannot know this, and so, when lies and stances are awkward, he goes out just the same to get as far as possible with the normal grips and swings. A foozle usually results, for it is not until the stroke is well on the way that he realizes that his balance is precarious and that disaster is coming.

On the other hand, there is another type of player who does not practice these shots but who takes no risks when they have to be played. For wood he takes, perhaps, a lofted iron, being content to recognize that the situation virtually has him beaten; he readily makes, as it were, a concession to it by playing for safety.

Now this is not the way to play first-class golf. If a full shot will reach the green, it must be seriously entertained. If the green be two shots away, the first shot should be sufficiently long and straight to bring the green within range of the second. Most good courses abound in this type of difficulty, and every one by practice should equip himself with the necessary knowledge to cope with it.

It has been pointed out elsewhere that we cannot study too closely the effect on the ball of changes of grip and swing. If the player will play quiet shots of, say, 5 yards—which he can well do indoors—and notice the effect of shutting and opening the blade, standing in front and behind the ball, striking horizontally and vertically, and so on, he will acquire a knowledge that will come to his aid instinctively when awkward situations arise. For big shots, so far as wrist and hip work are concerned, are merely little shots magnified, the principles involved being the same.

But one of the main benefits accruing from practice in playing awkward stances, etc., lies in this, that the player begins to recognize that more important than achieving length under such conditions is the ability to keep the ball straight; that until he can control the direction, length may really be a curse, for it may put him in the rough.

The instructions then set out for the guidance of those who propose to practice under these awkward conditions have in mind the twofold aim of keeping straight and getting length.

A.—Standing Below the Ball

(Fig. 140)

There are two usual cases. In the commoner one, the player is on an incline with the ball above him, in the other case he has a level stance in a depression. In neither case is the normal swing possible, for the ball is too high. Also, in the first case there is a difficulty in maintaining the balance; the tendency in the swing is for the center of gravity to shift in a direction away from the line of flight, that is, backwards down the incline.

The following modifications from the normal should be made:—

158

Stance—more behind, nearer the ball, slightly more open.

Grip—shorter, at bottom of the handle.

Weight—well forward on the toes, the body fairly upright.

Swing—more upright than usual.

NOTES

1. As balance is difficult to maintain, little pivoting is possible. The back-swing must be curtailed and fairly upright.

2. As length must be lost through the short swing, the player must over-club. A spoon is an invaluable club for this shot.

3. The shorter grip lowers the hands and tends to make the swing more normal. This is desirable, for accuracy of direction is important, and the more normal the swing, the more likely will direction be secured. The nearer stance enables the left to go through and tends to prevent the right from whipping over. A pull is the usual error in this stance.

4. The stroke, if with wood, must resemble that of an iron. There should be little hip-sway, and at impact, and throughout the down-swing, the forearms should be taut. The usual shot is of the nature of the push shot.

5. Finally, the player must endeavor not only not to fall away from the ball, but must endeavor to follow through with the left. If the swing be leisurely this can be done. A quick

159

swing is sure to result in a falling away from the ball, producing a short, feeble shot off the toe.

B.—Standing Above the Ball

(Figs. 141-2)

The conditions are the exact reverse of the foregoing. The player is tending to fall forward on to the ball, even in the stance and, of course, this tendency is emphasized immediately the swing begins.

The modifications in the stance, etc., suggested are practically the reverse of those suggested for A above:—

Stance—nearer than normal, ball midway between feet, slightly more square.

Grip—longer than usual.

Weight—more on left foot than right and well back on the heels.

Left Shoulder—braced, but lower than usual.

Swing—upright, but fairly loose.

Notes

1. Owing to the tendency to fall forward, it is best to adopt a crouching stance by bending the knees forward. This has the double advantage of bringing the hands nearer the ball and of keeping the center of gravity nearer the ground and so tending to preserve the balance.

2. The left shoulder cannot be brought round

in the back-swing, for the balance would be upset. Thus width is curtailed. Instead, a big lateral hip-sway must be made and the left arm movement will be fairly loose.

3. A lofted club must be used, e.g. the spoon for the brassie, mashie for the iron, and so on.

C.—PLAYING DOWNHILL
(Figs. 143-4)

In this case the right foot is higher than the left, and there is a tendency in the stroke to fall forward laterally parallel to the line of flight, that is, down the incline. Most weight is naturally on the left foot, in some situations it is practically all on that foot. That is the first variation from the normal. The second is the difficulty of making any but an upright swing, in some cases very upright, and of keeping a straight left leg.

The following modifications from the normal are suggested:—

Stance—slightly forward and open.

Grip—normal.

Back-swing—rather upright, but not more so than the lie compels.

Down-swing—down the incline, parallel to the ground.

NOTES

1. The forward stance enables the left hand to follow the ground in the down-swing: this

161

is essential. Extra length can be got by a forward fling of the body after the arms (Fig. 145). The tendency is to do the reverse, with the result that the arms come up again quickly after impact and length is lost.

If the stance has been well ahead of the ball, this forward sway is more easily accomplished.

2. The pivot tends to be restricted so far as the left leg is concerned, for in some cases it may be carrying all the weight. In this case reliance must be placed on a more pronounced lateral hip sway.

FIG. 145. — DOWNHILL STANCE, SHOWING CLUB-HEAD FOLLOWING SLOPE.

3. The ball is made to rise by using a more lofted club. The player must not attempt to get the ball up, the club will do that, his business is to strike down, following the ground (Fig. 145).

4. The back-swing should be no more upright than the lie of the ground compels; it is desirable at all times to get as much width as possible, for length will be lost in any case.

5. It is advisable to over-club and not to contemplate losing a stroke no matter how unpromising the lie and stance may be. After a few practice swings under such conditions the player will begin to realize that for this lie, about the

162

worst in golf, there is really a definite shot if he will prepare for it. He will certainly emerge from the ordeal with increased faith in the powers of his clubs.

D.—PLAYING UPHILL

(Fig. 146)

The conditions here are the reverse of those we have been discussing and the adjustments from the normal stance, etc., are also exactly the reverse:—

Stance—well behind.
Weight—more on the right.
Club—straight faced.
Swing—contracted back-swing.

NOTES

1. The tendency is for the weight to be on the right, the amount increasing with the slope. In the swing the tendency is for the body to shift down the slope and upset the balance so that a restricted back-swing is advisable, that is, there is little pivoting.

2. If the weight has shifted largely on to the

FIG. 145A.—PLAYING UPHILL.

right, there can be little follow through. A

163

see-saw movement of the shoulders is required to get the weight on the left at the top.

3. The stroke must be up the slope, not into the ground; hence the body must not be ahead of the ball, for the rising ground would impede the club-head. The stance must be well behind, so that after impact the club can swing up the slope.

4. To get as much length as possible, a straight-faced club should be used and it should also be on the side of power.

5. If the ball is lying on a very steep incline, which may be said to represent the limit of this kind of stance, the player should stand well behind and give it a left-handed blow with a stiff forearm, using a flat-faced club.

CHAPTER XXII

COMMON FAULTS AND HOW TO
CURE THEM

(Figs. 147-149)

THE faults dealt with in this chapter are the commonest in golf. Every one may be said to pull and slice occasionally in every round; some commit one or other of these faults at almost every hole. If they are only slight deviations from the straight line, there is little wrong and the errors will right themselves. Once the player starts altering his stance or grip or swing, the change produced is almost certain to do more than correct the error; a slice will probably give place to a wicked hook, a hook to a depressing slice, and so on, the remedy proving much worse than the disease.

But many players have spells of one particular form or other of these golfing maladies, and obviously some remedy is necessary in their case. It is for these unfortunate people that this chapter has been written. If the advice given does not appear to meet the case, the club professional should be consulted. He knows the player's physique, method of play, grip, stance, etc., and, being a trained observer, he should be able to lay his finger on the weak spot.

165

It does not follow that the advice in these pages is wrong; in all probability it has not actually been followed. It is not enough merely to endeavor to carry out these instructions when playing a round. The player must have it out with himself on a quiet part of the course. At first he will probably exaggerate everything he is advised to do, and so substitute one fault for another, a pull, say, for a slice. This is highly desirable, for it will convince him of the efficacy of the cure. Soon he will be playing well if he is an intelligent player and thinking keenly.

As a final introductory word, the player is urged to take particular note of his usual grip and stance and see if the error lies there. And he is further advised to swing at his usual natural pace.

SLICING

Cause 1: *Wrong grip.*

This may be contributory to the slicing habit but is unlikely to be the root cause. See that the grip is normal for the shot. For an ordinary drive two knuckles of the left hand should be visible and if the back of that hand is too much in front of the shaft it should be slightly altered, but very slightly.

The right hand grip should be as shown in Figs. 8, 9, 10. It should not be allowed to creep farther over the shaft.

Cause 2: *Too much weight on the left foot in the address.*

In the back-swing the club is brought too soon

166

round the body; in fact the left foot may be said to be the center of rotation. As a result the player is cramped at the top; the elbows are bent and the body is bent well forward throwing extra weight on the left foot. In the down-swing the player corrects this forward movement of the body by going back on to his right foot. Consequently, at impact, the club is cutting across the ball through inability of the hands to go through (Figs. 147-8).

Cause 3: *Shoulders too level in the address.*

This indicates that already the right is gripping unduly and has taken control. In the back-swing, the right lifts and the body leans forward on to the left foot.

The down-swing resembles (1) above.

Cause 4: *A stiff upright stance* (Fig. 13).

This is a common fault among lady players. There is scarcely any pivot and both sections of the swing are largely arm movements. The first movement in the swing is usually a backward sway of both the trunk and the head accompanied by a lift of the hands.

The hips appear to be locked in the address and to remain so, thus preventing either a hip swing or a shoulder movement. This is really the root of the trouble.

Similarly in the down-swing, the absence of body twist prevents the hands from going through and thus the club-head is brought inwards across the ball.

167

Cause 5: *Stance too open.*

The remedy in every case is the same, viz. get more width in the back-swing. Decide in the address that the back-swing is to be a dragging back as far as possible of the club-head along the line of flight, until the right hip has gone back to its braced position. If this movement has been consciously prepared for, or been actively in the mind, the faults of stance and grip mentioned above will remedy themselves.

In the down-swing, and especially at impact, the grip with both hands must be firm.

On no account start altering the grip so as to encourage a pull, that is, by putting the left hand more on top of the shaft and the right more under than is shown in Fig. 8. This may be a palliative but does not eradicate the disease. In this connection, as in any other, two wrongs do not make a right.

Tackle this disease firmly and do not pander to it by playing towards the left of the fairway. This practice only makes matters worse, for as the player does not intend the ball to go into the rough on the left, he instinctively, if not deliberately, cuts across it to get the slice necessary to finish on the fairway.

If there is difficulty in getting extra width, the player should, for a time, stand more square, for this will facilitate a wider back-swing. Also, at impact, he should be thinking keenly of his club-head and should have courage to roll his right

168

forearm in the follow through. He may pull horribly for a time, but the slice will disappear and a much longer ball will result. Firm up the grip, keep the head down and have courage.

PULLING

Cause 1: *A wrong grip.*

The grip is frequently contributory to the pulling habit, more so than to the slice. It is more natural for the right hand to get under the shaft than over the top and, usually, the players who grip habitually with the right in this way (Fig. 11) are right-handed players, that is, the blow is delivered largely by the right. With the hand in this position, the knuckling over at impact or just before is apt to be exaggerated, especially if the grip with that hand throughout the swing be very tight, as it is apt to be. The puller's grip, then, must be altered to the normal grip, suggested in Fig. 8.

Cause 2: *The right side is braced in the address.*

This throws undue weight on the right foot. The first movement is a draw away of the whole body along the line of flight, the right hand lifting but keeping the club-head shut.

The right hand is in control, but unlike the slicing positions, the right elbow is away from the body, as shown in Fig. 147. From this position it is difficult to get the elbow down to the position shown in Fig. 54, which is the proper position for a normal swing. Instead, it de-

169

scribes a circular outward arc, and the club-head comes on to the ball with shut face and the result is a pull from the very commencement of the flight.

Remedy.—See that the grip is normal and that the left hand has control. Let the grip with the right be slack in the address. Get width in the back-swing and keep the right elbow well in to the side. It ought to be noted in connection with pulling and slicing that the method of grounding the club in the address may have a distinct influence on the back-swing. Thus, if the club-face be open in the address there is a tendency to swing at once round the feet; thus width is lost, the left elbow bends, and a slice results. On the other hand, if the face be too shut, a pull may ensue.

It is best, in the long run, to address the ball with the club-face fairly shut, that is, with the toe well forward. This mode of address invariably tends to a wider back-swing and fuller pivot.

Topping, Ballooning, Dipping Right Shoulder, etc.

Cause: These are all symptoms of the same faulty back-swing already dealt with under Pulling and Slicing. The right hip has not moved laterally, the right hand has had control and the club has been lifted rather than slung.

At the top, the player feels mewed up. Both elbows are spread-eagled, and as there has been

170

little pivoting the player is conscious that the body is now cut out and that the down-swing is largely dependent on the arms and wrists. Consequently, the down-swing becomes a snatchy movement, as the arms are not actuated from a braced trunk.

Anything may happen. The club-head may hit the ground behind, and the caddie or partner on being appealed to will probably tell the player that he is dropping his right shoulder in the down-swing, as it is the most obvious thing to say. The real fault, of course, occurred in the back-swing and escaped notice.

SOCKETING WITH THE MASHIE

Cause 1: *The club is taken too much round the body in the back-swing.* This brings the left shoulder too far forward and the weight comes forward on to the left and stays there. An attempt to hit through the ball from this position sends the hands too far out from the center of rotation so that the club-head, at impact, is slightly outside the line of flight.

If the driver were in the hand, the same action would result in the ball being pushed out (not necessarily sliced).

Remedy.—Obviously the remedy is to get more width in the back-swing by taking the club-head back further along the line of flight. The player is again cautioned against addressing the

171

ball with the club-face too open, for this tends to a circular swing and so to an advanced left shoulder and bent left elbow. A see-saw movement of the shoulders is to be encouraged and the pivot should be restricted. This will help to prevent the left shoulder from coming forward towards the line of flight.

Cause 2: A narrow back-swing, leading to socketing, is sometimes due to *lifting with the right hand,* especially to an undue use of the right wrist. In this case the player's weight or center of gravity is advanced towards the line of flight and he is too near the ball when he tries to hit.

Remedy.—Bring the club back with the left until the right hip movement has been made and the hip has locked. Then lift the hands upwards, not round the body. This is the correct way to play all iron clubs: only from a back-swing made in this way can the player hit through the ball. Bringing the hands down towards the feet instead of outward towards the line of flight tends to prevent socketing, whatever the root cause of the trouble may be.

Cause 3: *Flicking the club-head just before impact.* This habit is the cause of other faults than socketing, such as hitting the ground behind and stabbing, and it is the prime cause of loss of length. It arises in the first place from the pernicious habit of playing short approaches entirely by the wrists. With a fine sense of touch

172

and responsive wrists, much delicate work can admittedly be done near the green by playing chips in this way, the body meanwhile being cut out of the stroke.

But mischief is bred by this habit. It may not show itself in the chips, but when the player is confronted with a shot, just outside the limit of his wrists, it comes out into the naked light. A hip swing and braced pivot are needed now to get length, whereas the player's mind is naturally centered on the wrists. The body movement employed is not a rhythmic hip-swing at all but an uncontrolled, unorganized body heave which may bring the shoulders forward towards the line of flight. Usually while the arms are going forward the body is actually swaying away from the hole (Figs. 38-39).

Remedy.—Cut out wrist work at impact with the mashie; avoid it like the plague. Keep the left shoulder braced and the forearm taut, and come back widely with the lateral hip sway. Then lift until the left shoulder stops the movement. Let the down-swing be a hip-swing and at impact firm up with the wrists, but don't flick. Strike down, not up. Power and control will at once be felt—power because the body is in the stroke, control because the blade is being allowed to put stop on the ball which it can very well do of itself.

Finally, then, whatever form the mashie weakness may take, adopt the advice given above and

173

put more faith in the club-head; it will not let the player down.

ON THE PUTTING GREEN

So many unaccountable and apparently stupid things are done on the putting green that he would indeed be a presumptuous man who claimed to have a remedy for every lapse. And although the symptoms may appear to be widely different yet they are generally traceable to two diseases, and these diseases in turn either to nervousness or carelessness.

In dealing with the mashie chip, the putt, and indeed with almost every shot, stress has been laid on the need for care in the address, and it is obvious that in so delicate an operation as putting, the details of stance and grip must be unusually important.

On the putting green the player is confronted with a peculiar problem. He is not asked to get length or control, he has to get exact length and exact direction and often he has to exercise specially great judgment through peculiarities of the green such as undulations, slopes, variations in length of grass, and so on.

Assuming that he has had considerable experience it is unlikely that, given normal conditions, he will make many errors of pure judgment. He may be too far or too short in his approach putts and wide with his short ones, but in practically every case this is due solely to faulty swings, that

174

is to say, to errors rather of execution than of judgment.

Now faulty execution can be traced back to two causes, viz. wrong grip and wrong stance.

Wrong Grip.—Many players, when about to make an approach putt, have felt at various times that they could not gauge the length, and that the stroke would be stiff and wooden. Perhaps they have felt that they could not determine how much the arms were to be employed in the stroke and how much the wrists. A little too much wrist, or a little too much push through and the ball would be away six feet or more past the hole. This is a tantalizing state of mind to be in but it is one that afflicts us only too often.

The cause of this condition is clear and the remedy simple. The body has been cut out of the stroke and this has arisen out of an unbraced grip. The remedy is exactly to reverse these conditions, that is, to cut the wrists out and to putt with the hips instead.

Whenever, then, a putt is to be made, the player should school himself in the details of the grip. Having placed his hands correctly, he must now brace up his shoulders and biceps. This will have the two-fold effect of imparting rigidity to the arms and flexibility to the hips. The stroke now becomes a hip movement. This will make the left shoulder dip in the back-swing and lift in the down-swing. If the arms are held rigid, a smooth, rhythmic and con-

175

trolled stroke should follow. This should be sufficient for all short putts, and for most approach
putts too. The extra wrist work required for
the longer putts will be applied automatically if
the player concentrates on the hip-swing.

Wrong Stance.—The occasions when a five-
foot putt is regarded with equanimity are very
rare. It has sometimes been urged that the best
plan is to go up to the ball and play it carelessly.
There is a world of wisdom in this, for it is only
another way of advocating a rhythmic hip-swing.
Let a player begin to take meticulous pains and
his legs and trunk will automatically stiffen and
a free stroke become difficult.

But the mental stress of a tricky approach putt
is apt to make the player adopt a forward stance.
Whenever this happens, the left shoulder invariably dips, so that the hands are not only in
front of the ball but they are dropped towards
the ground (Fig. 149). This is done quite unconsciously. It is impossible in that position to
make a backward sweep of the club-head along
the grass. The club-head must lift and, as the
arc described by the head in the downward
swing reaches its lowest point in front of the
ball, the stroke must become a stab, for the
club-head cannot come through if, at the last
moment, the player endeavors to push the club-
head through, it must go outside the line of
flight. The ball is thus hit on the heel and goes
to the right of the hole.

176

The remedy is to use an aluminium putter and to ground it before taking up the stance. This will tend to keep the body back. It may be said with much truth by the experienced, that counsels of perfection are apt to avail one little when a five-footer has to be tackled. That is readily granted, for temperament and ill-health may complicate the question, and the player may be rattled through having misjudged his approach. Concentration is not easy when the pulse is beating wildly and the soul is filled alternately with apprehension and remorse.

Many adopt a rather nonchalant pose and putt quickly, thinking that carelessness is less a fault than over-care; others, and there are many of them, fear to take pains lest they miss, feeling that failure in such cases carries added disgrace. Of course, the fault lies in taking trouble over the wrong things.

A good plan to adopt on all occasions is to take the proper grip and make a practice swing or two to see that the hip swing comes easily; then to walk up to the putt, whether long or short, and make it without fuss. There will, of course, be failures, but their number should steadily diminish. A good workman deserves credit always although fate may deny him success.

CHAPTER XXIII

WINTER GOLF

ONE of the greatest attractions of seaside links is their excellent playing condition in the winter months. It is true that at that period the wind may be additionally troublesome, but as a compensation the greens are usually less fiery and truer. But where the links specially excel at that season over inland courses is in the state of the fairways.

Seaside links are usually stretches of sand, partially covered with grass and heather, through which the heaviest of showers rapidly drain away. Thus the surface soil scarcely varies in consistency throughout the year.

On inland courses this is rarely so, except on chalk downs and moorland. As a rule, the surface soil varies from sand through gravel to clay, and its surface varies in hardness at different seasons. Thus a clayey course, which in summer has the consistency almost of concrete, may in winter resemble nothing so much as a glue-pot, so that in the former season a lofted shot rebounds wildly off the fairway while in the latter it may stay embedded in the turf.

It is obvious, then, that the method of play in

winter must vary very considerably from that in summer, for the changed conditions present problems that do not arise at other times. It would be well, then, to discuss some of these problems and try to evolve means of dealing with them. To battle with new difficulties may be the breath of life to some players, but usually winter golf is not a thing that members of inland courses eagerly look forward to. Many, indeed, put their clubs into winter quarters and wait for the drier and warmer days of spring before they venture again on the links.

Assuming, then, that the course is sodden, trouble begins immediately the tee shot is despatched. Usually it is difficult to get a good foothold and, as this is a prime essential to good play, the player must see that his shoes are fitted with large nails. It is not wise to wear thicker soles at this season and, although goloshes may keep the feet dry, it is against accuracy to wear them. If, however, goloshes are worn, they should be of the nailed variety. Rubber soles are unsuitable for wet, muddy stances.

The Ball.—The next trouble arises out of the ball. In winter the grass on the fairway is thin, and as there are few stubbles, the ball lies very closely: at this season worm-casts are unusually numerous, and so the ball may be barricaded on all sides by little mounds of earth. From a close lie on sodden or muddy turf, it is extremely difficult for the ordinary player to get the ball

179

up. Usually he drives it down into the wet ground from which it does not readily rebound. If the player be expert and at the same time a tremendous hitter, he may drive it through and up, but even then the ball has to be struck very fiercely to get a long carry, owing to the lowness of the initial trajectory. As a result, the majority of players fail to get the ball up and length is lost because the sodden ground curtails the run.

It is a mistake, then, to use a small, heavy ball in winter or wet weather, especially if the player be middle-aged or lacking in hitting power. A lighter and larger ball should be used instead; it is more desirable in every way. It sits up nicely and gives the player confidence, and has the further merit that it carries farther than the small, heavy ball. It rises more quickly, too, as the club can get more easily beneath its center. Not only does it carry farther but it runs less, through its higher trajectory, so that it is the better ball for pitching up to the green and, as we have seen, it is also the better ball for getting carry.

Clubs.—Stiff-shafted wooden clubs have a tendency to drive the ball low and so should be avoided by all, except the hard hitter. For winter play, therefore, whippy shafts are much to be preferred, for not only do they get the ball up but they give the player a better idea of the position of the club-head. And not only should the shafts be more whippy but the heads should be

180

slightly heavier. This arises from the fact that, owing to the poorer blood circulation, the player grips the club harder during the cold days and this naturally makes the club-head appear lighter. Some players, in winter, use drivers as much as 2 ozs. heavier in the head than their usual driver, to counteract the effect of the tight grip.

It is advisable, too, to use a heavier-headed brassie and spoon and to compensate by shortening the handle. The lie of the club should be more upright to enable the player to stand nearer his ball and so strike more accurately. This near stance is doubly desirable for, as has been pointed out elsewhere, the swing becomes more upright, as it has to be, to cope with the specially close lie. Both the brassie and spoon should have plenty of loft.

Shots.—In playing to the green from 120 yards or so, the pitch is the usual shot if the green be soft, for the ball can be played to alight on it and stop. It is unwise, however, to go on playing the pitch if the pitch-and-run be possible. The swing in the latter case is made slowly and has a pronounced follow-through, thus resembling a true iron shot. The pitch shot, on the other hand, is played faster with less follow-through and if a player persists in playing this stroke unduly, this method of play may creep into his iron shots with disastrous results.

CHAPTER **XXIV**

FROM TEE TO GREEN

As the young golfer has now been instructed in what is believed to be a sound method of playing the game, and of coping with some of its difficulties, it may perhaps be fitting to conclude with a chapter of advice on how to play a round.

No matter how well a player may be able to make all the ordinary shots in his practice spells, he cannot be called a golfer until he has gone forth and proved his skill under the stress of match play and competitive golf. Play under the latter conditions differs very much from practice spells, for the lengths are different and the lies and stances are usually different. Further, the player is highly conscious that the success of another shot hangs on the result of each shot he is attempting.

Of course, in these pages one cannot do more than advise in quite a general way on golfing policy. It is not thought that old heads can be put on young shoulders even if it were desirable, but it is well that wisdom, purchased by long experience, should be put on record that all who so desire may read, mark, learn and inwardly digest.

The following words are not written for that large band of happy, jovial fellows who make of a round of golf a social event. Nor are they in great part applicable to friendly matches. For all, however, who propose to compete in sterner engagements they should have more than a passing interest; and they may serve to show even the casual reader how absorbing the game of golf can really be and how great is the call it makes on those who strive to win distinction in its pursuit.

STROKE PLAY

This form of play is the hardest and best test of golfing skill, for from the first tee shot to the last putt the player is waging a remorseless struggle with the course.

If it be a four-round competition, he is not troubled much in the first three rounds about the doings of his competitors, but usually he begins the last round knowing that he must not exceed a certain score if he is to have the chance of winning. Sometimes, indeed, he may know the actual score that he has to make. With this exception, the player is not influenced by the play of his fellows as he is in match play, and is free to carry out any plan of campaign that appears to him to be best.

In some respects a stroke round resembles a game of chess. Each stroke is part of a definitely thought out plan, for in the making of it the

183

player has in view the best way of playing the next. No stroke is really good, no matter how truly hit, if it is at the expense of the stroke that follows.

Great concentration therefore is needed in stroke play, and as there is no opponent as in match play to bring the player up rudely by his brilliance and so change his tactics, he is usually free to work out his own ideas. It is seldom wise for him to be influenced by the play of his partner. It may be, for example, that the latter is doing brilliant work with a certain club and habitually using it. It would be unwise to imitate him.

It is an advantage to play with a successful opponent, for a run of good luck on his part reacts favorably on one's self, whereas one cannot be oblivious to his bad luck or bad play and is apt to be depressed and unhappy about it.

Practice Rounds.—The practice rounds prior to a big competition should not be strenuous. The ideal practice partner is a man of wide experience, for he may bring to the problem wise and original ideas. After each hole the player should consider which is the best direction from which to approach the hole, for that is the critical stroke. In this connection he will note not only the disposition of the bunkers but also such conformations of the immediate approach as may affect the run of the ball. For example, some greens are so contoured that they gather up approach shots from certain quarters and

184

spurn them if from others: thus in such cases the placing of the previous shot is a matter of great importance.

It is advisable to get plenty of bunker practice, especially near the green, so as to become familiar with the tenacity of the sand. Nothing is more disconcerting than a misjudged niblick shot.

Some players, in their practice rounds, go all out to test their form, but this is rather unwise, especially if they are playing well, for failure to reproduce this form in the opening round of the competition proper is apt to rattle them. It is the same inevitable tendency to institute comparisons that so often leads players to make a mess of things in competitions on the home course. It is a good plan not to hole out.

If the caddie has shown good judgment, his advice may be followed at times, but usually it is best in the competition proper for the player to follow his own judgment. For he knows his own plan and what he can do with each club; above all, he knows which club is giving him best results. "Never change a winning game" is a good motto in sports; and "Never change a winning club" is a good motto in golf. If there is a wind, it is important to note its effects on the tee shots, for the shot to the pin may become a very difficult proposition if proper allowance for the wind is not made. On many seaside courses the wind may blow from the opposite point of the compass on successive days, and it is well to be prepared with a stroke plan in the event of such a change.

On the Tee.—A spot should be selected to drive at, and the player should look at it steadily for a moment or two to impress it on his consciousness and then take up his stance with reference to it. If he keeps this spot in his mind throughout the stroke, he will be able to impart that definiteness and decision to his wrist work that is so desirable in the follow through.

Here it may be interpolated that in golf generally, and in stroke competitions in particular, success comes not solely because the strokes are good, but because they are precisely what was intended. Nothing spurs on a player so much as the growing consciousness that he has control of his clubs.

To come back to the player on the tee. It is a good plan to divide the fairway up mentally into three parallel strips. If there be out-of-bounds on either side of the fairway, he should tee up on that side and drive to a spot on the middle strip. This is much the safest plan. Suppose out-of-bounds were on the right, and the player were to tee up on the left. He would be conscious that the slightest pull would put him in the rough, and the slightest slice out-of-bounds. There would be an inevitable tendency to slice out-of-bounds; in consequence, the tee shot would prove anything but easy to play. If the player is a long hitter, the chances are that the tee shot from such a quarter would be disastrous.

Through the Green.—As he advances to his ball, the player should be considering how and with what club it is to be played. But there must be a plan: long before he reaches the ball, the player must have decided upon the strength of the shot with whatever club he is compelled to use. To leave this question to the last minute is wrong. One must be getting up an attitude of mind, a fixity of purpose, a comprehensive view, if one is to succeed; to play each shot detachedly, to play in units, as it were, seldom leads to success, for it fails to build up the winning mood and spirit. Experienced golfers know this and, if following as spectators, refrain from distracting a player by attempting conversation between the shots.

If the ball is lying unfavorably, an adjustment in the plan may have to be made. If it is a three-shot hole, requiring normally a drive, brassie and mashie, it will be necessary to decide how the length can still be got without risking a foozle. Probably it will be best to play first a nice easy mashie or a mid-iron. This is not playing pawky. The soundness of this course lies in this, that a player feels he is playing well if he gets good value for his shots and is apt to improve through added confidence. Therefore, in the first few holes especially, those clubs should be avoided which, while suited to the length,

187

are unsuited to the lie. This is really good advice. Any other course may lead to a foozle which, while disconcerting in itself, is apt to lead to further trouble. The player begins to press to recover his lost ground, to attempt carries, perhaps, that are beyond him, and generally to commit various errors of judgment that result from a bad beginning.

Assuming, however, that the lie is satisfactory, the player is free to play as he had predetermined. It may be a difficult shot, perhaps a wee bit risky, but if it will gain a stroke advantage over a pawky shot, it must be attempted. Suppose, for example, it is a difficult carry over a cross bunker guarding a green lying just beyond. To play short would be a definite concession of a stroke to the course. That would be bad policy, to acknowledge defeat half-way. The policy is for the player to go for it, having faith in his normal golfing ability to bring off the shot. If he fails, he can still get on from the bunker, and he has the feeling that he very nearly brought it off and may do so next time. His bad luck will not depress him nearly so much as bad play or over care.

Philosophy goes a long way in golf, and the player should recognize that by the law of averages the bad luck of the first few holes will be made up by good luck later on. The Spirit of the Course may have got him into one or two bad lies and tempted him into one or two

188

bunkers, but the player will get level presently by bolting a few putts and dodging by hair-breadths some very bad trouble. What he has to avoid above all things is attempting a shot that requires more favorable conditions of lie and stance than those before him, for such a course is sure to bring discomfiture.

One or two points may be mentioned here on method of play. Whenever a bunker has to be carried, a golden rule is "Hit down, and keep the head down." Also, if a player cannot concentrate, a full shot is less likely to bring disaster than a spared or controlled shot, for he needs only to shut his mental eye and strike. But this practice will not bring success. The player must place and he must control, and the requisite frame of mind to do this is what he must gradually work up to by discipline and judgment, and it won't come by playing full shots.

Another point has to be mentioned here, although it has been referred to over and over again in this book. A stroke should never be made speculatively; the player should know exactly what he wants the ball to do. If a speculative shot succeeds, it brings little solid comfort; if it fails it brings certain remorse.

When a player proposes to play from a bunker, he should have reckoned up what are the possibilities of the position. If the green is accessible from the bunker, he should aim to reach it and should weigh up carefully his chances of doing so: it should be his chief aim. If a niblick will not reach, he should consider the advisability of trying a mashie. If, however, the green is a full shot away, he should undoubtedly concentrate solely on getting out, for there is nothing to be gained by taking risks in that case. He has lost a shot by getting into the bunker and, unless he gets out, may lose two. In this case he will consider the advisability of playing back or sideways. Also in a bunker a player can scarcely hit too hard; usually he is too timid.

On the Green.—Some courses, notably championship courses, have very large greens which, towards the end of a summer competition, are apt to become threadbare and shiny. Three putts are frequently required, especially if the approach putt is from a remote corner of the green. It is a matter of real difficulty, not to say luck, to lay an approach putt dead from such unusual distances under these peculiar conditions. And the short putt, probably three yards, requires only the slightest of taps to propel it to the hole. Undoubtedly the best policy for holing the short putt is to go for the back of the hole firmly, otherwise the ball will almost certainly slide past the hole. There is not enough bite on the grass to steady it and keep it straight. If the ball hits the back of the hole fairly, it will drop; at worst, it will swing round and lie dead.

190

Timidity loses more strokes under such conditions than boldness.

At any time and under any conditions, the club should not be grounded until the player is about to strike, for any subsequent movement of the ball may involve him in the loss of a stroke.

MATCH PLAY

On the tee the player should have mapped out how he intends to play the hole; where the drive is to be placed, where the second, and so on, and he should endeavor as far as possible to adhere to this plan. The body always reacts to the predominant stimulus, and there is a great danger, if the plan is suddenly changed, of a shot mis-carrying through lack of concentration, through failure to get the original thought entirely out of the mind. One is too apt to think that his play must be guided by that of the opponent.

Of course, the play of the opponent cannot be ignored, but it should be allowed to alter one's tactics very little. Suppose it has been proposed to carry a distant bunker requiring a perfect shot, and the opponent's play makes it unnecessary to take the risk through his failure, perhaps, to reach, it is generally unwise to play pawky. This is most especially true if one is playing well. A player should always play up to his own standard and never descend to the oppo-

191

nent's level. This is not solely because the level of the latter's game may at any time rise, but because by playing pawky one becomes for the time being some one else, some one inferior to one's true self. The opponent's good play ought to make one play better, but his bad play should not be allowed to make one play worse. Playing pawky seldom pays in first-class golf. But apart from the depressing effect that one's own good play may have on the opponent, by which is meant one's skill rather than exercise of discretion, it is really essential to play to the best that is in us if the best that is in us is to be brought out.

Another aspect of careful tactics is to be considered, and that is the possibility of the opponent making a brilliant recovery. A player is then placed in the disconcerting position of having to play something very good to get on level terms, and every player of experience knows that this is very difficult to do if it happens that he has been playing for keeps.

It is generally admitted to be an advantage to out-drive the opponent, for, by watching him play the odd, one may learn much about the strength required, the effect of the wind, and one learns, of course, how he has fared.

But playing the like has its disadvantages. Suppose he has put the odd near the pin; this cannot fail to be disconcerting to most players and to become more so the longer they look at

192

it. The player must resolutely ignore the ball or it may unconsciously affect his plans; if it is slightly beyond the pin, he may decide to be not so far and so be woefully short, or if it is short of the pin, he may be led to over-run.

If the player is himself playing below form, he will in that case have to alter his stroke plan; he is now in turn playing the rôle of second fiddle. One cardinal rule to adopt is to try not to run the risk of playing two unfortunate shots in succession. Suppose, for example, the drive is in the rough and the second to the green over a bunker, which was originally to be carried, has become now somewhat uncertain. In that case, an easy second should be played with a view to reaching the green with the third. This careful shot will restore the player's self-esteem and confidence and will still keep him in the running. If the opponent lays his second dead, he is reaping his just reward and the policy has not been proved in error; if he comes to grief or lies wide of the pin, it may be said to be justified. It is well to remember, that although the opponent may be outplaying one through the green and may gain a stroke, it is quite easy for him to lose his advantage on the green.

On the green one is in rather intimate contact with the opponent and deliberation appears to indicate a personal determination to down him. Do not make the mistake of pitying your opponent if things have fared ill with him, for it begets a flabby frame of mind and your own game may begin to deteriorate. It is always a very difficult thing to maintain a winning lead by one's own excellent play, for the tendency is to slow up, to have mercy, so to speak. This is a fatal attitude to adopt. It is apt to show itself most of all on the putting green when a putt that one might reasonably be expected to hole has to be made to win 'the hole. The temptation to make no fuss about it and to make certain of a half is often too strong to be resisted, and in this way the advantage gained up to the green is thrown away. Many games have been lost on the green through a player squandering his profits in this way. Never putt for the half if there is a reasonable chance of holing.

A word may be said here about etiquette. The sum total of the rules is thoughtfulness for the opponent. Never express an opinion on the probable result of any of his strokes. If you wish your opponent to putt out, stand by and keep silent; if you do not wish him to putt, say so definitely. Do not say: "Oh, you can't miss that," or "It's your hole," or some such phrase, for he may putt half-heartedly and miss. He won't thank you if you subsequently tell him you had already given him the putt, and he certainly won't if you proceed to profit by his slip.

Bogey.—This form of play resembles match play in that the result is settled hole by hole,

194

but in other respects varies widely from it. One is not worried, for example, about the opponent's score, for one knows beforehand what the colonel will do. This is essentially a form of game in which it is advantageous to work to a stroke plan and to go out for everything. It is true that one is competing against not only the bogey but also the field, and it is well, if things are working out according to anticipation, to try to bolt every putt for wins, because one is always able to putt freely for the subsequent half if one over-runs five feet. This freedom on the green accounts for the remarkably low stroke scores that are sometimes brought in on a bogey card.

Bogey competitions are not very common in first-class golf, and they always appear to be in the nature of a consolation race for the erratic; for the player who can play well and badly alternately. It is not to be inferred from this that such players usually win but only that they come nearer to winning than they ever do in stroke competitions.

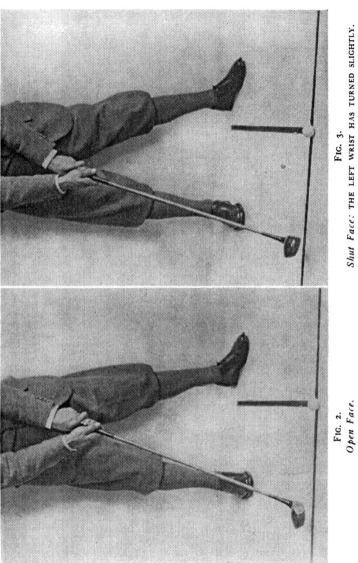

FIG. 2.
Open Face.

FIG. 3.
Shut Face: THE LEFT WRIST HAS TURNED SLIGHTLY.

GRIPS.

FIG. 6.
Correct Grip for Left Hand: PRESSURE IS ON FIRST JOINT OF THUMB—WRIST ACTION IS FREE.

FIG. 7.
Incorrect Grip for Left Hand: PRESSURE IS ON BALL OF THUMB—WRIST ACTION IS RESTRICTED.

FIG. 8.
Vardon or Overlapping Grip: LITTLE FINGER OF RIGHT HAND OVERLAPS FIRST FINGER OF LEFT. THE LEFT HAND GRIPS AS SHOWN IN FIG. 6.

GRIPS.

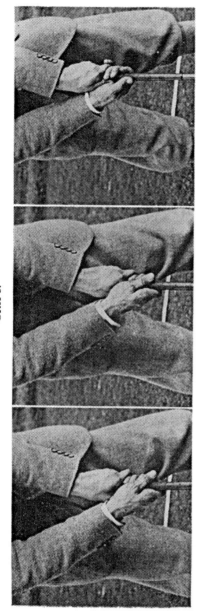

FIG. 9.   FIG. 10.   FIG. 11.

FIG. 9.—MITCHELL'S DRIVER GRIP.
FIG. 10.—MITCHELL'S IRON GRIP: THE GRIP IS MORE IN THE FINGERS.
FIG. 11.—*Incorrect Grip:* BOTH HANDS ARE TOO MUCH TO THE RIGHT—THE RIGHT HAND SHOWS TOO MANY KNUCKLES
AND THE LEFT IS TOO FAR UNDER. THIS IS A "PULLER'S" GRIP. THE BACK-SWING WILL LACK WIDTH.

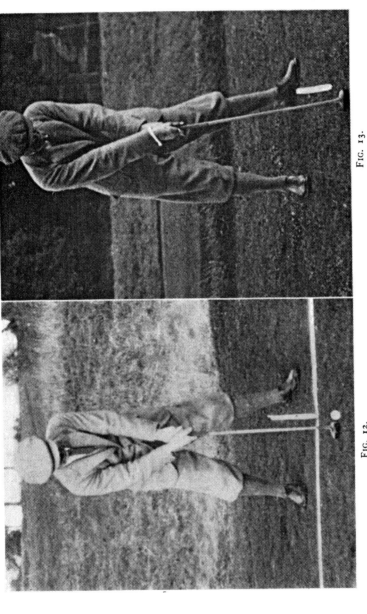

Fig. 12.

Correct Address for Drive: LEFT SHOULDER UP AND BRACED, RIGHT KNEE BENT SLIGHTLY TOWARDS BALL, RIGHT SHOULDER DOWN, RIGHT ELBOW NEAR RIGHT HIP.

Fig. 13.

Incorrect Address for Drive: RIGHT ARM AND SHOULDER BRACED, RIGHT LEG STRAIGHT AND RIGHT SHOULDER UP, ARMS OUT FROM BODY, WRISTS ARCHED, RIGHT ELBOW AWAY FROM RIGHT HIP.

FIG. 14.—*Correct Stance:* RIGHT KNEE BENT, HANDS DOWN, RIGHT
SHOULDER DOWN.

FIG. 15.—*Incorrect Stance:* RIGHT KNEE UNBENT, HANDS AWAY FROM
BODY, RIGHT SHOULDER UP, WRISTS ARCHED.

FIG. 16.

FIG. 17.

FIG. 18.

Initial Movement in the Back-Swing.

FIG. 17.—*Correct.* THE MOVEMENT HAS BEEN FROM THE HIPS DOWNWARDS—THE HIPS HAVE MOVED LATERALLY—NO PIVOT.

FIG. 18.—*Incorrect.* FEET AND LEGS TOO RIGID—NO LATERAL BODY MOVEMENT—SHOULDERS AND TRUNK HAVE TURNED— THE RIGHT HIP MOVEMENT HAS BEEN CIRCULAR, THROWING WEIGHT ON THE HEEL—FINISH SHOWN IN FIG. 39.

FIG. 19.   *Initial Movement in Back-Swing (from Films).*

FIG. 20.

FIG. 19.—*Correct.*   CLUB-HEAD STILL MOVING ALONG LINE OF FLIGHT—HIPS HAVE SWAYED LATERALLY.
FIG. 20.—*Incorrect.*   TRUNK HAS TURNED—RIGHT HIP CANNOT LOCK—NO POWER.

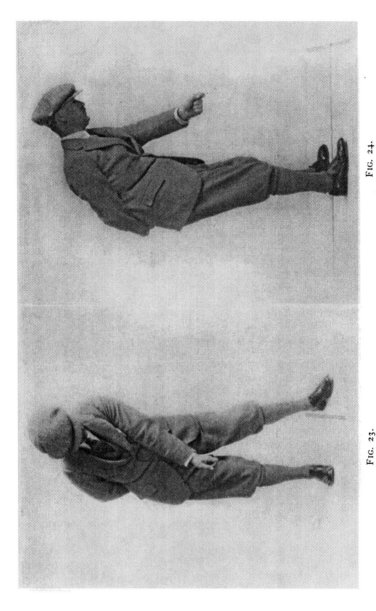

FIG. 23.

FIG. 24.

Correct Initial Movement in Back-Swing: SIDE VIEW (FIG. 23), BACK VIEW (FIG. 24). THIS LEFT-HANDED MOVE-MENT IS RECOMMENDED AS SUITABLE INDOOR PRACTICE. NOTE STRAIGHT LEFT ARM—ABSENCE OF PIVOT—PRONOUNCED LATERAL SWAY OF RIGHT HIP—LEFT WRIST ACTION.

FIG. 25.   *Incorrect Initial Movement in Back-Swing.*

FIG. 26.

COMPARE THESE POSITIONS WITH FIGS. 23 AND 24. NOTE ESPECIALLY PREMATURE TRUNK TWIST AND PIVOT IN FIG. 26.

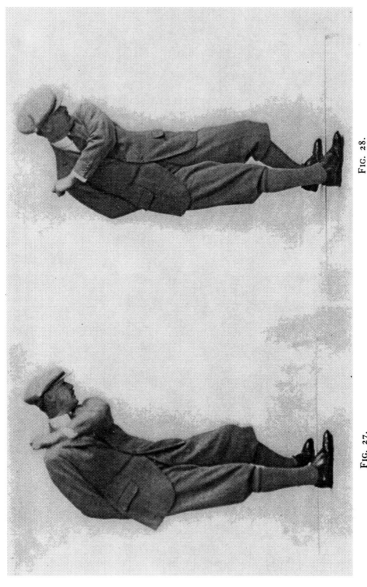

FIG. 27.

Correct at Top: PLAYER CAN HIT DOWN AND THROUGH —WEIGHT CHIEFLY ON TOES—THE PIVOT IS CONTROLLED FROM THE RIGHT HIP.

FIG. 28.

Incorrect at Top: NOT ENOUGH SEE-SAW—UNCONTROLLED PIVOT—LEFT SHOULDER TOO HIGH—POWER GONE OUT OF ARM—CANNOT HIT DOWN.

FIG. 29.

FIG. 30.

FIG. 31.

FIG. 29.—MUSCLES ALONG THE BLACK LINES ARE BRACED, AND RESISTING
THE PIVOTAL TWIST.

FIG. 30.—*Correct at Top:* NOTE STRAIGHT LEFT ARM—THE LATERAL SWAY
—PARTIALLY SHUT CLUB-FACE. START OF THIS SWING WAS
FROM THE FEET.

FIG. 31.—*Incorrect at Top:* NOTE CIRCULAR SWAY OF RIGHT HIP—UN-
CONTROLLED TRUNK MOVEMENT—BENT LEFT ARM. THIS
SWING WAS FROM THE HIPS—UPWARDS.

FIG. 36.

FIG. 37.

Correct at Impact.

IN BOTH FIGS. THE LEFT SHOULDER IS UP AND THE ARM STRAIGHT. THE PLAYER IS HITTING "AGAINST" THE RIGID LEFT LEG, WHICH IS RESISTING THE TENDENCY OF THE BODY TO GO FORWARD. (Cf. FIGS. 38-39.)

FIG. 39.

FIG. 38.

Incorrect at Impact.

BODY HAS DRAWN AWAY FROM HOLE—THERE IS NO FOLLOW THROUGH—SLICED BALL RESULTS—WEIGHT IS STILL ON THE RIGHT LEG. MASHIE APPROACHES OFTEN GO WRONG THROUGH THIS ACTION. (SEE FIGS. 36-37.)

FULL DRIVE (WITH SLIGHT FOLLOWING WIND).
FIG. 41.   FIG. 42.

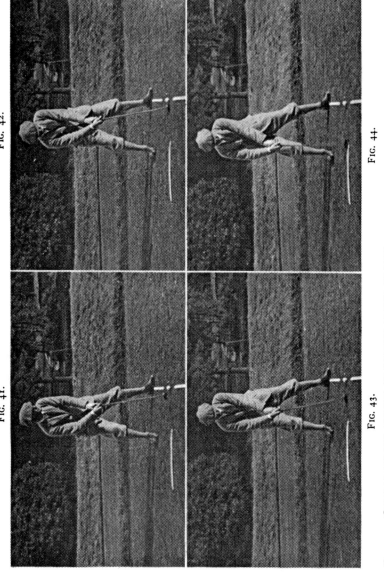

FIG. 43.   FIG. 44.

FIG. 41.—GETTING MENTAL PICTURE OF PROPOSED FLIGHT OF BALL.
FIG. 42.—BRACING UP THE MUSCLES AND GETTING THE "IMPACT" FEELING (PAGE 54).
FIGS. 43-44.—HANDS MOVING AHEAD OF THE CLUB-HEAD—LATERAL HIP SWAY NOTICEABLE BY OBSERVING TREE IN BACK-
GROUND—NO PIVOTING.

FULL DRIVE—*Continued.*

FIG. 45.

FIG. 46.

FIG. 47.

FIG. 48.

NOTE ABSENCE OF PIVOT UNTIL HANDS BEGIN TO LIFT (FIG. 48).

FULL DRIVE—*Continued.*

FIG. 49.

FIG. 50.

FIG. 51.

FIG. 52.

NOTE ARMS GO ROUND WITH THE SHOULDERS—THAT IS, DO NOT GAIN ON THE SHOULDERS. WHEN THE LEFT SHOULDER IS HELD BY THE HIP (FIG. 50) THE ARMS CEASE TO ROTATE AND LIFT. RIGHT LEG IS FIGHTING HARD BELOW THE KNEE AND TWISTING—NOT SWAYING—ABOVE. NOTE STRAIGHT LEFT ARM AND PARTIALLY SHUT CLUB-FACE.

FULL DRIVE—*Continued.*

FIG. 53.

FIG. 54.

FIG. 55.

FIG. 56.

HIPS ARE UNWINDING AHEAD OF THE SHOULDERS—LEGS ARE SPLAYED AND BODY HAS DIPPED GROUNDWARDS.

FULL DRIVE—*Continued.*

FIG. 57.

FIG. 58.

FIG. 59.

FIG. 60.

HIPS ARE SQUARE TO LINE OF FLIGHT IN FIG. 57, AND THE SHOULDERS IN FIG. 60. BOTH KNEES ARE BENT TOWARDS HOLE JUST BEFORE IMPACT.

FULL DRIVE—*Continued.*

FIG. 61.

FIG. 62.

FIG. 63.

FIG. 64.

Swinging Against a Firm Left Leg: RIGHT SHOULDER IS DOWN AND RIGHT ARM STRAIGHT—RIGHT WRIST IS WHIPPING OVER THE LEFT, WHICH IS ALSO ASSISTING IN THE MOVEMENT. NOTE MOVEMENT OF RIGHT HAND RELATIVE TO LEFT IN FIGS. 63, 64.

FULL DRIVE—*Continued.*

FIG. 65.   FIG. 66.

FIG. 67.   FIG. 68.

Relaxing: NOTE THAT THE BALANCE HAS BEEN KEPT AND THAT THE LEFT HIP DOES NOT TWIST OUT OF THE WAY UNTIL WELL AFTER IMPACT.   (CF. FIGS. 62-63-64 WITH FIGS. 65-68.)

FIG. 70.—*Spoon Shot.*

Note SHORT GRIP—SHORT BACK SWING—RESTRICTED PIVOT OWING TO EARLY
LOCKING OF RIGHT HIP. FROM THIS POSITION THE DOWN-SWING WILL BE
MORE VERTICAL THAN USUAL WITH WOODS, I.E., MORE LIKE THAT OF AN
IRON.

FIG. 74.
STANCE FOR A SLICE.

FIG. 75.
STANCE FOR A PULL.

FIG. 77.
Down-Wind.
WEIGHT MORE BEHIND BALL—
SLIGHTLY MORE OPEN

FIG. 78.
Against Wind.
FAIRLY SQUARE—SHORT GRIP.

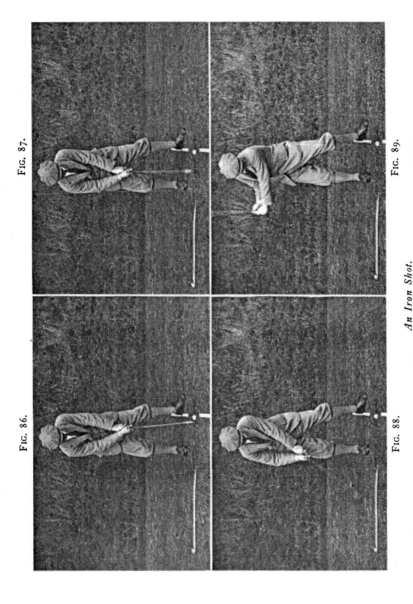

FIG. 87.

FIG. 86.

FIG. 89.

FIG. 88.

An Iron Shot.

Note: (1) LATERAL SWAY OF RIGHT HIP (FIGS. 87-88), AND THAT HANDS LEAD. (2) NO SHOULDER MOVEMENT UNTIL THE HANDS LIFT (FIG. 89). THE SWING HAS BEGUN AT THE FEET, AND EXTENDED UPWARDS TO THE HIPS.

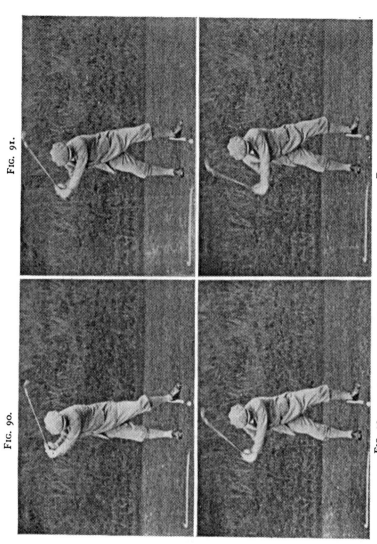

FIG. 90.

FIG. 91.

FIG. 92.

FIG. 93.

THESE FIGURES ARE VERY INSTRUCTIVE AND ILLUSTRATE IMPORTANT POINTS IN IRON PLAY:—1, A STRAIGHT LEFT ARM THROUGHOUT; 2, THE HIP TWIST IS AHEAD OF THE SHOULDERS; 3, SPLAYING OF THE KNEES; 4, DEFERRED WRIST ACTION.

FIG. 95.

FIG. 94.

FIG. 97.

FIG. 96.

1. RIGHT ELBOW HUGS THE SIDE (FIG. 94) AND RIGHT ARM IS STRAIGHT AT IMPACT AND AFTER.
2. STRAIGHT LEFT LEG AT IMPACT.
3. THE CONTINUOUS UNWINDING OF THE HIPS.
4. WRIST ACTION IS CONFINED MAINLY TO THE SECTION OF THE SWING SUCCEEDING THE FIG. 94 POSITION.

FIG. 99.

FIG. 98.

Short Running Approach.

Note: THE STANCE—LEFT KNEE BENT FORWARD TOWARDS LINE OF FLIGHT—ABSENCE OF PIVOT—EXTENDED ARMS KEEPING BALL LOW—SHUT FACE IMPARTING PUSH AND TOP SPIN (FIG. 99)—SLIGHT ROLLING OF WRISTS (FIG. 98).

FIG. 100.

FIG. 101.

FIG. 102.

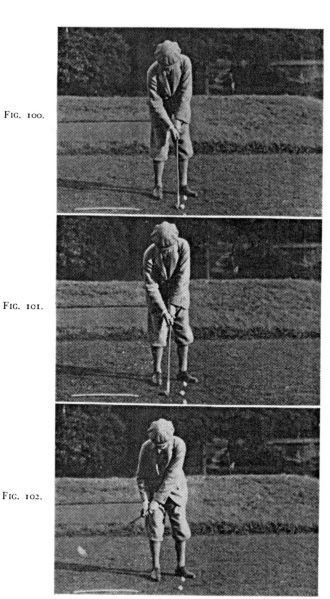

Mashie—Pitch-and-Run.
(130 YARDS, WITH RUN OF 30 YARDS.)

FIG. 103.

FIG. 104.

FIG. 105.

Mashie—Pitch-and-Run.

Note: ABSENCE OF HIP PIVOT (FIG. 103).
  TURN OF SHOULDERS HAS BEEN MADE AGAINST A STRONGLY
  BRACED RIGHT HIP, GIVING GREAT CONTROL.
  STRAIGHT LEFT ARM THROUGHOUT.
  LEFT SHOULDER BROUGHT SQUARE BY UNSCREWING RIGHT
  THIGH.

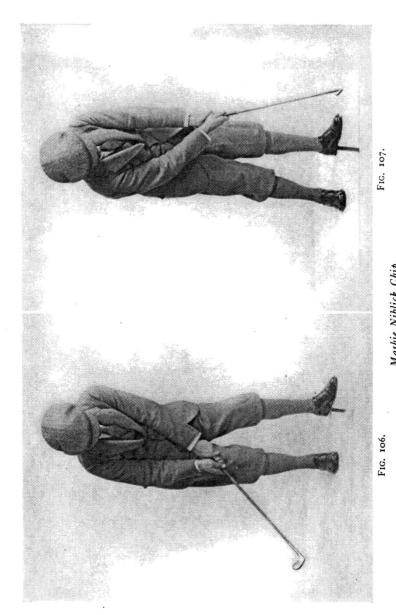

FIG. 106.

FIG. 107.

Mashie Niblick Chip.

FIG. 106.—BEGINNING OF SWING—CLUB-FACE SHUT—HIP
SWAY—NO HIP OR SHOULDER PIVOT. FIG. 107.—AFTER IMPACT—CLUB-FACE OPEN—LATERAL
HIP MOVEMENT TOWARDS HOLE.

Fɪɢ. 109.

Fɪɢ. 108.

Mashie Pitch.

Fɪɢ. 108.—*Correct* INITIAL MOVEMENT—CLUB-FACE SHUT AND FOLLOWING LINE OF FLIGHT—NO HIP PIVOT.
Fɪɢ. 109.—*Incorrect* INITIAL MOVEMENT—CLUB-FACE OPEN AND AWAY FROM LINE OF FLIGHT—HIP PIVOT.

FIG. 110.   FIG. 111.   FIG. 112.

Mashie Niblick Pitch.

THIS IS A HIGH LOFTED SHOT OF ABOUT 90 YARDS—PERHAPS OVER TREES.

Note: STANCE—FIRM RIGHT LEG RESISTING SHOULDER MOVEMENT (FIG. 111)—OPEN CLUB-FACE AND BODY WELL BACK (FIG. 112).

FIG. 113.

FIG. 114.

FIG. 115.

Mashie Pitch—130 Yards.
(TO DROP ON THE GREEN.)

FIG. 116.

FIG. 117.

FIG. 118.

COMPARE 116 WITH 105—THE HANDS AND SHOULDERS
ARE FURTHER BEHIND THE BALL FOR THIS PITCHED
SHOT.

FIG. 120.

FIG. 119.—*Finish of Pitch:* HANDS FORWARD AND LOW AND CLUB-FACE
OPEN.
FIG. 120.—*Finish of Pitch-and-Run:* CLUB-FACE SHUT—BODY FORWARD.

FIG. 123.   FIG. 124.

Cut Shot from Rough Grass.
(GREEN 20 YARDS AWAY OVER RAVINE.)
Note: OPEN STANCE—VERY OPEN CLUB-FACE (FIGS. 121-22)—HEEL OF CLUB LEADING AT IMPACT (FIG. 123)—LOW FINISH. NOTE REMARKABLE SIMILARITY OF FIGS. 121 AND 123. THESE FIGS. ARE SELECTED FROM A FILM.

FIG. 127.   FIG. 128.

FIG. 129.   FIG. 130.

Bunker Shot.

Note WIDTH (FIG. 129) AND OPEN STANCE. THE CLUB-HEAD HAS TAKEN
A NATURAL COURSE ACROSS THE LINE TO THE PIN, THE RIGHT SHOULDER BEING
KEPT LOW (FIG. 130). SEE ALSO FIG. 124. NOTE DISTURBANCE OF SAND.

FIG. 131.   FIG. 132.

FIG. 133.   FIG. 134.

On the Putting Green.
(SIX-FOOT PUTT.)
Note: BALL IMMEDIATELY BENEATH EYE—UNMOVED RIGHT ARM AT END OF
BACK-SWING (FIG. 133)—UNMOVED LEFT ARM—THAT THE PUTT WAS A HIP-
SWING WITH REST OF BODY TAUT AND RIGID.

FIG. 140.—*Standing Below Ball.*
Note: BRACED LEFT SHOULDER—
SHORT GRIP—
RESTRICTED PIVOT AND
SWING.

FIG. 141.—*Standing Above Ball.*
Note: BENT KNEES—WEIGHT
KEPT LOW.

FIG. 142.—*Top of Swing Above Ball.*
Note: LONG GRIP—SHORT SWING—
RESTRICTED PIVOT.

FIG. 143.—*Playing Down-Hill.*
NOTE FORWARD STANCE—RESTRICTED
PIVOT—SHORT GRIP.

FIG. 144.—*Playing Down-Hill.*
BODY HAS GONE FORWARD.

FIG. 146.—*Playing Up-Hill.*
STANCE WELL BEHIND—SHORT GRIP—
VERY RESTRICTED PIVOT AND BACK-
SWING—CLUB-FACE SHUT.

FIG. 147.

Wrong at Top: ARMS SPREADEAGLED—TOO MUCH WEIGHT ON LEFT.

FIG. 148.

Wrong at Top: SEE FIG. 66 FOR CONTRAST.

FIG. 149.

Wrong Putting Stance: HANDS AND BODY TOO FAR FORWARD—CLUB-HEAD CANNOT GO THROUGH.

CPSIA information can be obtained at www.ICGtesting.com
Printed in the USA
BVOW01s1847221113

337072BV00008B/294/P